Tactics for Trout

TACTICS
FOR
TROUT

Dave Hughes

Illustrations by Richard Bunse

Stackpole Books

Copyright © 1990 by Dave Hughes

Published by
STACKPOLE BOOKS
Cameron and Kelker Streets
P.O. Box 1831
Harrisburg, PA 17105

Printed in the United States of America

10 9 8 7 6 5 4 3 2 1

First Edition

Cover design by Tracy Patterson with Caroline Miller
Cover photograph by Jim Schollmeyer

Library of Congress Cataloging-in-Publication Data

Hughes, Dave.
    Tactics for trout / by Dave Hughes; illustrated by Richard Bunse.
    p.   cm.
    Includes bibliographical references (p. 218).
    ISBN 0-8117-2403-4
    1. Trout fishing. I. Bunse, Richard. II. Title.
  SH687.H764   1990
    799.1'755–dc20   90-9488
                                            CIP

To my editor, Judith Schnell, without whose wisdom this book would not have been written.

Contents

Introduction

I watched wistfully from my viewpoint at the riffle's head while Rick Hafele and Jim Schollmeyer fished the riffle's tail. Trout and laughter spilled into the air down there. They were catching fish and having fun. I wasn't catching any fish, and I wasn't having much fun.

Half an hour earlier we had pulled the drift boat to the bank at the edge of the long riffle in the Bighorn River, in south-central Montana. I had shot off upstream. The water was shallower up there; I could fish my nymphs without the addition of split shot and strike indicators, which at that time I mildly detested. I figured I'd catch a few fish, Rick and Jim would catch a few more fish than I did, and all three of us would arrive back at the boat happy. That's the way it usually went.

That isn't the way it went this time. I ran through the contents of a full box of nymphs, trying everything from a #16 Pheasant Tail to a #10 Gold-Ribbed Hare's Ear without feeling a single tap that told of a take. That wasn't enough action to make me happy, especially when every glance downstream revealed another trout dancing in the air.

I edged down toward them.

A few minutes later I stood fishing between Rick and Jim, my ears assailed by a barrage of advice, my leader encumbered with an indicator and a couple of split shot. After working the kinks out of my casting, caused by all of the gadgets between me and the #16 Pheasant Tail I was ordered to tie on and try again, I finally hooked a trout. It was close to a couple of pounds, which isn't big for the Bighorn. But it puffed me up to have a trout and some laughter of my own bouncing around in the air above the riffle.

The search for the right fly, which I'd gone through at the head of the riffle, often hinders the process of finding out what trout really want, which is what Rick and Jim accomplished at the other end of the riffle.

They knew that the right presentation is just as important as the right pattern. You'll catch a few fish by using the wrong fly with the right presentation, since the wrong pattern presented the right way still looks like a living thing to a fish. But you won't catch many trout using the right fly with the wrong presentation. It won't look alive at all.

You'll catch the most fish when you select the best pattern for the situation and use a presentation that is appropriate for the chosen fly. *When pattern and presentation are in agreement with each other, and in agreement with what the trout want at the moment, then you will begin catching more and larger trout.* That is the goal of *Tactics For Trout.*

By the next day on the Bighorn I believed myself to be an expert at fishing nymphs with indicators and split shot. I slipped the boat ashore at the same long riffle, this time with my brother Gene and his friend Dick Johnson aboard. Both were relative beginners at fly fishing. I put them in the same water that we had fished the day before, rigged them the same way, and within a few minutes had both into fish. Their success increased my cockiness.

I left them and waded up to the shallow head of the riffle where I had fished without indicator and split shot before edging down to take lessons from Rick and Jim. I rigged with a light split shot, adjusted my indicator lower on the leader, and tied on the same #16 Pheasant Tail I had used in the same water the day before. Half an hour later I had taken only two fish. I might have waded out of the riffle slightly deflated, but my indicator popped under one more time.

This one was an 18-incher, an ancient brown with battered fins and a frayed tail. It didn't look like the kind of trout that would be satisfied with #16 groceries, but there was the pesky nymph pinned in its lower lip. I knew then that it was not the fly, but the way the fly got shown to the fish, that fooled the fish into making its mistake. The same fly fished in the same water the day before, without the indicator and shot, had not drawn a hit. I unpinned the nymph, let the old trout slip away, and waded out of the riffle with my ego reinflated.

Gene and Dick and I drifted down a lot of beautiful river and enjoyed some fine dry-fly fishing over an afternoon hatch of Little Olive mayflies before my ego got deflated again.

It was evening before the Little Olive duns stopped and the trout quit rising to drys. But this presented no problem: in my new role as both guide and expert, I merely advised Gene and Dick to switch back to the same nymph tactic that had worked earlier in the day. They did. For an hour in the failing light they cast their nymphs and watched their indicators and hoped something would happen. Nothing did. I tried it, too, casting confidently at first, then a bit hurriedly, and finally almost frantically as the last light fled. Our nymphs were absolutely ignored by the trout.

It was almost dark, past time to make the final reel-up and run to the boat ramp. But I wanted Gene and Dick to end the day with fish tugging at the ends of their leaders. In a move that had some desperation in it, but was not without reason, I had them strip the indicators and split shot from their leaders and fish their Pheasant Tail nymphs on downstream swings.

I showed them how to mend line at intervals to keep the flies from swimming too fast. It was the exact method I had used the morning before, the method that had failed so brilliantly while Rick and Jim took turns taking trout. But this time I knew there would be lots of Little Olive nymphs, damaged while attempting to emerge and still trapped in their shucks, washing down with the current.

Within a few minutes Gene hooked a fish. He played it, landed it, released it, and reeled up. He waded out and we leaned against the side of the drift boat talking quietly while Dick kept on casting and fishing his fly on the swing. I was about to call out to him to move down the riffle a few feet, to cover a new slice of water, when he shouted into the darkness and a trout squirted into the air.

The simple downstream tactic had taken fish for both of them and had worked a wonder for me.

A tactic that is exactly right for one situation is often exactly wrong for another. *The key to trout tactics, and therefore the key to successful trout fishing, lies in knowing the full range of methods that work with dry flies, nymphs, wet flies, and streamers, and being able to call on the one tactic that is right for the fishing situation in which you find yourself.*

In *Handbook of Hatches* (Stackpole Books, 1987), a companion book to this, I wrote in detail about fly pattern selection based on the foods that trout eat. In *Reading the Water* (Stackpole, 1988), the second book in the series, I wrote about the variety of water types and how to find trout in each of them. In *Tackle and Technique For Taking Trout* (Stackpole, 1989), the third book in the series, I wrote about trout tackle selection and the wide range of fly casting techniques.

This book, *Tactics For Trout*, covers a wide range of trout fishing methods. It will help you combine your knowledge of trout foods and fly pattern selection, your ability to read water and find fish, and finally your balanced tackle and casting skills into a specific tactic that completes the connection between the fly and the fish.

I hope it helps you fill the air with trout and laughter.

Part I
About Trout

1

Trout Species

Trout fishermen pay little attention to trout. We study tackle and tactics. We study trout foods and the flies that match them. But we seldom study the trout themselves. I am guilty of this. I have pressed my nose to the pages of so many books about aquatic insects that I can tell you more about the life cycle of the phantom midge than I can about the brown trout that swirls to take it.

Trout evolved from marine species that lived in the Arctic Ocean back when the earth was warmer. During the ice ages these ancestral fish moved south away from the ice and returned north again as the earth warmed and the ice melted.

Early brown trout and Atlantic salmon migrated out of the Arctic Ocean through the gap between Norway and Greenland. Browns nosed down the coast of Europe and spread throughout the rivers of Europe and into Asia. Atlantic salmon followed both shores of the Atlantic Ocean: Europe on the east and North America on the west. No salmonids spread beyond the equator until man transported them to the southern hemisphere in the 1800s.

Brook trout migrated down the east coast of North America, probably advancing and retreating several times at the urgings of various glacial ages. They became the native trout on our eastern shore, with populations spreading inland to the Great Lakes region and the vast area that drains into Hudson Bay.

Rainbow and cutthroat trout, along with the related Pacific salmon, migrated out of the Arctic Ocean through the intermittent opening at Bering Strait between Alaska and Siberia. At times this was a land bridge, allowing species such as the camel and horse to migrate from America to Asia, and later such species as man to step from Asia onto our own landmass. When it was open water, as it is now, the ancestors of our current western trout species swam through it and nosed southward along the west coast of America and the east coast of Asia.

Our understanding of the evolution of trout species and subspecies is in its relative infancy. Much of what we knew in the past was based on fossil records and speculation about species migrations. Much of what scientists are learning today is based on studies of trout genetics.

The new knowledge is tossing some of the old out as wrong. For example, the rainbow trout has always been classified in the genus *Salmo* with browns and other trout. Recent DNA studies reveal that the rainbow and a Pacific salmon native to the Soviet Union's Kamchatka Peninsula are the same species. The Asian salmon was named *Oncorhynchus mykiss* before our own rainbow was named *Salmo gairdneri.* So, according to the rules of taxonomy, the rainbow now takes the older name and suddenly becomes a salmon instead of a trout.

But this won't change the way the rainbow swims, the way we fish for it, or the way it pops out of the water when stung with a hook.

BROOK TROUT

The brook trout, *Salvelinus fontinalis,* is the native trout of the east. Until the late 1800s it was the only trout in the settled parts of the North American continent. It is actually a char, closely related to the Arctic char, Dolly Varden, and lake trout.

The brookie is dark green on the back and dorsal fin, with

Brook trout *Jim Schollmeyer*

vermiculations that look like lines in a wormwood maze. The pectoral, ventral, and anal fins are pink to reddish, with white stripes on the leading edges. The belly varies from creamish white to burnt orange. The underside of the male sometimes turns crimson or even black at spawning time. The sides have numerous yellowish spots, with fewer red spots that are surrounded by blue haloes. The tail is only slightly forked, hence the common name "squaretail."

The record brook trout weighed 14½ pounds and was taken from Ontario's Nipigon River, north of Lake Superior, in 1916. Brookies are still taken annually that tug scales to the 8-pound mark, but only in the remote northern parts of their range. Anything over a 5-pound fish is exceptional. The average size gets smaller as one moves from north to south in their native range. In Canada 1- to 2-pound fish are typical, but in New England and the eastern United States 6- to 9-inch trout are caught more often, and a 1-pound fish is a big one.

Brookies have strict habitat requirements, needing cold, clear water. They do better if the water is slightly acidic. They do not survive in waters that reach temperatures above 75°, and do not do well in waters without some sanctuary that remains below

65°. They are extremely susceptible to trouble caused by logging, farming, and pollution.

In most of their original habitat in the United States, brook trout are now relegated to tiny headwater streams and forested mountain lakes and ponds. The typical fish in such waters is small, but as pretty as the tiny waters from which it arises.

The native range of the brook trout extends from the Arctic Circle south to Appalachian headwater streams in Georgia. The inland range reaches streams in Manitoba and the Great Lakes states of Michigan and Wisconsin.

The brook trout does not survive well in hatcheries and is costly to raise for planting. It is not a leaping fighter like the rainbow and is considered stupid when set alongside the wary brown trout. Consequently, it has not been used extensively as a stocker. As its preferred habitat has dwindled, the brook trout has been displaced by hardier rainbow and brown trout.

Brookies have been transported to many high lakes and streams in the Rocky Mountains and the far West where they find favorable conditions and do very well. They have also been introduced in Europe, Asia, New Zealand, and Argentina. Brookies are excellent fish for remote plantings in lakes that lack spawning tributaries; they are the only trout species that spawns with more than mild success in stillwater, establishing self-sustaining populations without further plants. In some lakes, especially in the high-mountain West, they overpopulate and become stunted.

Because of their gullibility, especially when small, brook trout need remoteness and lack of fishing pressure to produce good populations of fair-sized and larger fish. That is why they are a wilderness fish, whether they are found in the north or in the mountain regions of the West. A few trophy brookies are now taken in the West, usually from lakes. But most trophies are still caught in large rivers draining into Hudson Bay and Ungava Bay in northern Quebec.

Brook trout have an anadromous life cycle wherever they have access to salt water, moving out to salt water for long periods to feed, then returning to fresh water to spawn. They average about 4 pounds. There are a few runs of sea-run brookies along the coast of Maine, though most are found in Labrador and Quebec.

Brook trout are not held in high regard as fly-rod fish. They are strong, but not leaping fighters. They have a reputation for stupidity, earned by their willingness to take bright wet flies that look like nothing in nature. They also have a reputation for being bottom feeders, and therefore poor dry-fly fish. But they feed on the surface when surface food is floating about, and can be taken on drys as easily as any other trout.

Perhaps Joe Brooks best summed up the nature of the brookie when he wrote, "They zip up from their shelter beside or under a rock, hit, and if you don't hook them, turn and dash back, all in a second, a fleeting flash of wild trout." That describes the brookie as he is known to most of us: a fleeting flash of wild trout.

CUTTHROAT TROUT

Cutthroat are the native trout of the west. They followed the rainbow's reclassification, and are now *Oncorhynchus clarki* rather than the earlier *Salmo clarki*, which makes them a Pacific salmon. They have not heard about it, though, and not one of their characteristics has changed.

All cutthroat are characterized by the features that give them their name: the two red slash marks on the underside of the lower jaw. There are many subspecies, displaying various colors and spotting patterns, some not unlike the rainbow. It is best to

Cutthroat trout *Jim Schollmeyer*

identify them by the red slashes, which all cutt subspecies possess and which rainbows lack.

The record cutthroat was a 41-pound specimen taken from Nevada's Pyramid Lake in 1925. It belonged to a genetic strain of the Lahontan subspecies, adapted to the specific conditions of its vast lake, and typically growing to great size. Irrigation diversions on the Truckee River blocked spawning migrations of these salmon-sized cutts, and the strain that carried the genes for that immense growth is now believed to be extinct.

Most very large cutthroat are taken from lakes. A typical stream cutthroat in most of the West would measure 10 to 14 inches. A nice one would reach 20 inches and weigh between 3 and 4 pounds.

Cutthroat are distributed along the West Coast from northern California to Prince William Sound in Alaska. Their origins are in coastal watersheds. The cutthroat's migratory routes took them all the way from the Pacific Ocean across the Continental Divide into the Yellowstone River, and from there into isolated headwaters in such places as Arizona and the Bonneville Basin in Utah. Tracing these routes is a scientific detective game with its clues hidden in geologic events, fossil evidence, and minute differences in DNA

Like brook trout, cutts are gullible and therefore susceptible to heavy fishing pressure. They don't compete well against more aggressive species that have been introduced, and their ability to tolerate pollution is low. Logging, grazing, land development, and mining have reduced habitat and taken a toll on stocks of native cutthroat.

The species is fragile in hatcheries, making it more costly to raise than the sociable rainbow. This cost, added to a reluctance to jump when hooked, has kept them out of demand as planted trout. As they have been caught and taken out of their native waters, they have been replaced by rainbows.

Cutthroat spawn in late winter or early spring, often in waters still running with snowmelt. They do best in cold, clean water, and need clean gravel beds. They do not spawn in stillwater, though an inlet stream that appears to be insignificant can sometimes populate a pond or lake.

Wherever they have access to the ocean, cutthroat have an anadromous life cycle. Many remain resident in fresh water, but most drop down and spend at least some time in salt water. Sea-run cutthroat have been recorded weighing as much as 17 pounds, but a pound or two is more typical. Sea-runs are wary and take to the air when bitten by a hook. They are excellent fly-rod fish.

The geography of the West was still forming as cutthroat dispersed inland. Consequent strandings left isolated populations that adapted to the waters in which they lived, eventually displaying unique characteristics, and there are now many distinct subspecies. The coastal race, *Oncorhynchus clarki clarki*, is apparently the oldest in the cutthroat line, and the trunk from which other subspecies slowly branched.

West-slope cutthroat, *Oncorhynchus clarki lewisi*, are found primarily in the western drainages of the Rockies in Idaho and Montana. The Yellowstone cutt, *Oncorhynchus clarki bouvieri*, is the most abundant pure cutthroat strain left in the interior. The fine-spotted Snake River cutthroat has yet to be given a scientific subspecies name. Its native range is limited to the Upper Snake River in Wyoming, above Palisades Reservoir. The true Pyramid Lake Lahontan cutthroat last spawned in 1938, and the strain is now thought to be extinct. But other Lahontan strains, *Oncorhynchus clarki henshawi*, survive in their native waters and in waters where they have been transplanted.

A few other cutthroat subspecies are represented by relict populations in a few isolated headwaters. These include the Humboldt cutthroat in Nevada, the Paiute cutthroat in a single stream in northern California, and the Greenback cutthroat in Colorado.

Like brook trout, cutthroat are primarily insect eaters, but take smaller fish as opportunity presents itself. As a fly-rod fish, the cutthroat is probably best represented by the sea-run strain on the coast, the Yellowstone and fine-spotted subspecies in Montana and Wyoming, and the trophy fisheries for Lahontan cutts where they have been stocked in trophy lakes from California's Martis Lake to Washington's Lake Lenore.

RAINBOW TROUT

The rainbow was originally classified as *Salmo irideus* in honor of its coloring. That was changed to *Salmo gairdneri* in honor of

Rainbow trout *Jim Schollmeyer*

the naturalist who first collected and described the species. In 1988 its name was changed again, to *Oncorhynchus mykiss,* a reflection of origins that are closer to those of the Pacific salmon than they are to those of the Atlantic salmon and brown trout.

Rainbow trout can be identified by their dark backs, silver sides, and liberal dashing of small spots on the sides, tail, and back. A red band runs along the lateral line, though it can be very faint on bright specimens. Their gill covers are often blush-colored.

The rainbow apparently arrived after the cutthroat, but being a hardier fish it displaced the cutt in many waters and drove it into marginal habitats in others. Cutts had already colonized many interior waters before geological barriers isolated them. Dispersion of the rainbow was halted by these same barriers. It is not commonly understood that the rainbow is a transplant in the Rocky Mountain states of Montana, Wyoming, and Colorado, states deservedly famous for rainbow fishing.

The sea-run form of the rainbow is the steelhead. The rainbow in almost all of its genetic strains retains a strong affinity for the sea. Even where the ocean is not a possibility, rainbows will follow their instincts to move downstream. They are spring spawners.

The original range of the rainbow extends from the Aleutian Island chain to northern Mexico, and along the Kamchatka Peninsula in the Soviet Union. Before man and dams and pollution arrived, steelhead ran upstream and spawned in most clean, cold streams with access to the Pacific Ocean. Their range extended far inland into Idaho, where steelhead swam hundreds of miles to spawn in the Clearwater and Salmon rivers, tributaries to the Snake River that flows into the Columbia River. Some steelhead still make the trip despite all of the dams.

Rainbows are fast-water fish. They prefer cold, tumbling streams, and are more apt to be caught in riffles and runs than in still pools. They are extremely adaptable, though, accepting habitat conditions that would distress or kill a brookie or cutthroat.

Because of their adaptability, they do well in hatcheries and have been planted almost everywhere. McCloud River stock from California were transferred to the Great Lakes in 1876, where they caught on and became a steelhead fishery that exists to this day. They were introduced to eastern streams not long afterward. The same stock became the seed for the fairy-tale fisheries in New Zealand, Argentina, and Chile.

The greatest drawback of the rainbow, in terms of planting, is its strong tendency to migrate, which makes it more a short-term investment than a long-term, self-sustaining cure for an ailing fishery. But they are the fish most likely to be used as put-and-take hatchery trout.

The record rainbow weighed more than 42 pounds, was taken near Ketchikan, Alaska, in 1970, and was a winter steelhead, not a resident fish. The record fly-caught rainbow weighed 33 pounds, was taken from the Kispiox River in British Columbia, and was a summer steelhead. The largest resident fish are nearly always taken from lakes. Average stream rainbows run 10 to 14 inches. Anything from 2 to 4 pounds is a nice fish. A rainbow that weighs more than 5 pounds should be bragged about no matter what kind of water it comes from.

Rainbow trout are excellent fly-rod fish. They are not as gullible as the brookie or cutthroat, but they do most of their feeding on the kinds of small organisms – aquatic and terrestrial insects – that are perfectly imitated with flies. They are ready feeders on both naturals and imitations.

BROWN TROUT

The brown trout, *Salmo trutta*, is both our oldest and newest trout. It is a European fish. The history of fly fishing is closely intertwined with it. The origins of the first sophistications in tackle, tactics, and fly patterns, most of which occurred in Britain, can be traced to the desire to please the demanding brown trout. But the brown is the newest trout in North American waters.

A typical stream brown runs 12 to 16 inches long. Any brown trout over 20 inches long and weighing more than 3 pounds should connect you directly to the great age of the species and the long history of fly fishing for it.

Browns can be identified easily by their bronze to yellowish brown coloration. They have numerous black spots on sides, tail, and back, and fewer but larger red spots on the sides.

The original range of the brown trout includes most of Europe and much of western Asia. It is native to the Mediterranean basin, the Black Sea and its tributaries, Iceland, Afghanistan, Lapland, and even the Atlas Mountains in Morocco. Many closely related species are spread across southern and eastern Europe and Asia.

Brown trout first arrived in America in 1883 as a shipment of eggs from Germany. There was a subsequent infusion of eggs from Scotland, which explains the old thinking that the brown

Brown trout *Jim Schollmeyer*

was actually two species: the German brown and the Loch Leven brown. They are the same species from two sources.

Browns were established in many eastern rivers of the United States before the turn of the century. In the next few decades they became the dominant fish in most heavily fished eastern waters. Many anglers at the time decried their presence, blaming the decline of native brook trout on them. But this was sour grapes: the fragile brookie was killed off or driven into marginal headwaters by man's meddling, not by brown trout. The hardier brown was able to supplant the brookie because it was able to withstand the pollution, silting, and warming of waters that killed brookies.

Another reason for the dim view of the brown: early American tactics had been worked out on the easily caught brookies, but they didn't work on the difficult import. Brown trout nudged American fly fishermen toward the same refinements of tackle, tactics, and fly patterns that this fish had encouraged in Britain, and for the same reason – in order to catch them more consistently.

The brown trout has been transplanted all over the world, wherever there are trout streams. The lake fishery of Tasmania, off the south coast of Australia, sports brown trout. Some of the best fishing in New Zealand is over selective European browns. South America offers some of the best brown-trout fishing in the world today.

The brown is not an easy trout to raise in hatcheries. But the brown lacks the rainbow's urge to run toward the sea, and is a good long-term investment rather than an abrupt put-and-take proposition, where the trout must be caught within weeks or be wasted. Brown trout thrive in waters warm enough to stress other trout. They are able to spawn, and therefore create sustaining populations, in waters that are too slow and silted for the rainbow.

Browns are thought to be more predaceous than other species of trout, taking more than their share of trout fry and fingerlings. In a way it's true: more browns avoid getting caught, and therefore live long enough to attain the size at which all trout species become predators of their own kind.

Brown trout spawn in fall or early winter. They become active then, shifting around more than at other times of the year, and become more vulnerable to the fisherman. In rivers that flow into lakes, big browns nose out on migratory runs toward spawning beds, sometimes when the water is low and fishable. Most trout species spawn in spring when rivers are high with snow-melt. The brown trout's spawning timetable creates the opportunity to take a fine trophy when fishing conditions are prime.

There is a sea-run form of the brown trout in its native range, although there are very few sea-run brown populations in North America. Some streams in Chile and Tierra del Fuego, at the tip of South America, offer excellent sea-run brown fishing.

The brown trout is, perversely, considered the perfect fly-rod fish because of its reluctance to take flies. It feeds on all of the natural foods imitated by artificial flies: aquatic and terrestrial insects, small crustaceans such as scuds, and baitfish. But it is highly selective, creating challenges in imitation, tackle refinement, and presentation skills. It is the fish that keeps dedicated anglers returning to difficult rivers.

Browns feed readily at the surface, taking perhaps a higher percentage of food there than other species of trout. They are excellent dry-fly fish. Their fight is not as aerial as that of the rainbow, though many do jump and all are strong, excellent fighters. But it is the challenge of getting a brown onto the hook, rather than its antics after it has taken the fly, that draws us to it.

GOLDEN TROUT

Golden trout are the most beautiful of our trout species. Native only to the Kern River basin in northern California, they are of rainbow derivation, hence their scientific name, *Salmo gairdneri aquabonito*, now changed to *Oncorhynchus gairdneri aquabonito*. They were cut off early in the evolutionary cycle of the western trout species and adapted over the ages to their tiny environment. Their beauty almost surpasses that of their Sierra surroundings.

Goldens are brilliantly marked. The back is greenish, the sides yellow-gold with a crimson band running the length of the lateral line through a series of dark parr marks. Cheeks and belly are bright red or deep orange. Black dots contrast like ink spots on tail and back. Ventral, caudal, and dorsal fins are tipped with white separated by a bold black band.

Found originally only in their Kern River basin, goldens have been successfully transplanted to high streams and lakes, most from six to ten thousand feet in elevation, in almost all western states. The record golden weighed 11 pounds and was taken from a Wyoming lake in 1948. Typical stream fish are 6 to 8 inches long. Any golden over 15 inches long and weighing more than a pound is a very nice fish.

Golden trout are related, at least in terms of the manner of their arrival and stranding far back in time, to other relict populations of trout. These include the Mexican golden trout, *Oncorhynchus chrysogaster,* of the Sierra Madre Mountains, the Gila trout, *Oncorhynchus gilae,* from the Gila River in southern New Mexico and Arizona, and the Apache trout, *Oncorhynchus apache,* from the White Mountains of Arizona. All are speculated to be more closely related to rainbows than to cutthroats, but it is not yet known exactly when all of the braches of western trout separated.

DOLLY VARDEN TROUT

The Dolly Varden, infamous for its supposed passionate gobbling of salmon, steelhead, and other trout young, has had an unfair finger pointed at it. It is part of the char genus and has been called a western form of the eastern brook trout, to which it is related. The Dolly, *Salvelinus malma,* is tangled with its close relatives the Arctic char, *Salvelinus alpinus,* and the bull trout, *Salvelinus confluentus,* which has only recently been listed as a separate species. The scientific clarification has not filtered down to become common knowledge yet. It is clear that studies revealing the Dolly to be a ferocious piscavore were based on both the Arctic char and bull trout. The Dolly Varden is actually the least predaceous of the three. But this information is not likely to clear its bad name in a hurry.

Dolly Varden trout have a native range from eastern Siberia across Alaska to the MacKenzie River delta in northern Canada. A subspecies ranges south to waters emptying into Puget Sound in Washington. The northern part of this range overlaps with that of the Arctic char. Because the latter fish has a better reputation, if less deserved, records have been kept for Dolly Varden under the name Arctic char. Tourist interests are afraid that fishermen would not make expensive fly-in trips to fish for mere Dolly Vardens, so they continue to call them by the more glamorous name: Arctic char.

The former record Dolly was a 32-pounder caught in Lake Pend Oreille, Idaho, in 1949. But that record fish is now known to have been a bull trout, and the current record is a 17-pound Alaska Dolly Varden – listed as an Arctic char. It's confusing.

The largest true Dollies are of the sea-run form, and reach weights in the 15- to 18-pound range.

I added my own notes to the confusion about Dolly Varden in my recent *Reading the Water.* The 6-pound Dolly that I reported catching in Oregon's Metolius River was actually a bull trout.

2

Trout Senses

Trout don't munch their meals at a table in a closed room, protected from the rest of nature by the walls and roof of a house. They exist in immediate contact with the things they eat and things that eat them.

Trout are predators. To exist they must find and capture prey just as surely as a pride of lions must winnow the weak from a herd of wildebeest. Trout fins are not claws; trout have no means to dismember large victims into bite-sized pieces. Each thing a trout eats must be small enough to swallow whole.

Because its world is well populated with aquatic insects and small crustaceans, and at times enriched on top with a sprinkling of terrestrial insects, these are most of what a trout eats until it grows to such size that it can swallow sculpins, dace, and other baitfish. Even then, most trout continue to take most of their nourishment from smaller bites: insects and crustaceans.

A single wildebeest feeds a whole pride of lions, perhaps for a couple of days. But it takes a lot of small bites to fuel a trout for a single day. The quest for food is almost constant. There are periods, even during midsummer days, when trout do not feed, seeming to lie dormant. But these periods are usually tied to a lack of opportunity, not to satisfaction. Trout don't sit around patting their bellies and burping. When food is available it trips a trigger and trout feed. They normally continue to feed with eagerness until the opportunity has gone.

Trout are predators, but they are also prey. When some insect or other activity prompts them to feed, it generally draws them out of cover and into exposed positions, where they are more vulnerable to osprey, otter, and man. Whenever trout are exposed they are wary, and therefore harder to approach and to fool with a fly.

Trout live by the success of their senses and die because of their senses' failure. In order to get trout attached to a hook, it is first necessary to get past their defenses, moving into position and presenting a fly without alarming them. Second, it is necessary to charm them into believing that fluff of fur and feathers is something they would like to eat.

TROUT VISION

From the angler's point of view, a trout's vision is its most critical sense. The effects of vision are two-pronged. First, a trout sees or does not see the fisherman as a threat. Second, a trout sees an artificial fly either as something good to eat or something to flee from in fear.

Trout do not see in exactly the same way we do. In our eye, light rays pass from air into liquid and bend; the cornea on the outside is round, the iris on the inside flat. We can focus only in a narrow line of sight and must move our eyes to bring whatever we want to see into the center of our vision. In the trout's eye, light passes from liquid to liquid, the outer cornea is flat, and the inner iris round. As a result, trout have 180-degree vision in each eye and can bring anything within that arc into focus.

Each of our eyes is connected by nerves to both sides of our brain. Like a pair of binoculars, we can focus and concentrate on only one object at a time. Each of a trout's eyes is connected to just one side of its brain. It can, therefore, focus on one thing with one eye, another with the other eye, like two independently

roving monoculars. Add this ability to the 180-degree arc of
vision in each eye, and you can see that a trout can observe a
wide range of objects over an extreme field of view. This means a
trout can focus one eye on an insect or an artificial tumbling
awash into its feeding territory while focusing the other eye on
some blurred but brightly vested object it considers a potential
predator.

A trout obtains binocular vision in the narrow area where the
field of vision from both eyes overlaps. Binocular vision allows
perception of depth of field and therefore permits measurement
of distance. It allows the fish to gauge range and intercept a
drifting insect or a baitfish scooting through its territory. It is no
accident that the trout's binocular vision is placed precisely in
front of its mouth.

The price paid for this slight field of binocular vision in front is
an angle of similar size behind with no vision at all. Fish almost
continually swim facing into the current. You should be aware
that the trout's blind spot is almost always straight downstream
from its position, directly behind it.

A trout can focus at extremely close range: an inch or two.
This, again, has an advantage and a price. The trout can scruti-
nize with care whatever it is about to make into a meal. But
when both eyes are focused on food so near, there is no way to
watch out for predators. When a trout holds and feeds within a

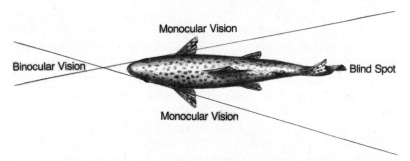

Trout have 180 degrees of monocular vision with each eye, binocular
vision in front where vision of the two eyes overlaps, and a blind spot
directly behind where they cannot see at all.

few inches of the surface, usually during a heavy hatch, its close focus reduces its ability to perceive a potential danger. That is why, with proper caution, you can approach to within fifteen or twenty feet of them. That is also why you must present your flies right into their feeding lanes. They won't move two or three feet to take a fly because they can't see it that far away.

A trout's eyes remain focused at short range unless something jerks its attention into the distance. What would do that? Such things as a bright hat looming on its narrow horizon, the brisk weaving to and fro of a thin stick, or the flash of sun from a fly line overhead. Any of these things would startle a trout, cause it to shift its focus from near to far, and make it poise to flee.

The implication is obvious: keep your movement to a minimum. Approach visible trout, or potential holding lies, slowly and with smooth movements. It is surprising how close you can move to a fish if you ease yourself into its field of view.

Color

It has been argued that trout cannot see color. The argument still goes on, but experiments have shown that trout can be taught to take food from a blue forceps and avoid it when offered on a red forceps, or the opposite. Scientists have even shown that trout can distinguish between shades of the same color.

This has its meanings both in the way trout see the angler and in the way they see the flies an angler tries to feed them. An angler in bright clothing is more visible to fish, and more likely to frighten them, than an angler wearing dull colors that blend with the background. An artificial fly is more likely to be accepted if it fits in with the general run of what trout eat most of the time. If trout feed selectively on a specific insect or crustacean, a fly that captures the color of the natural is more likely to be taken for the real thing.

The wrong color on the angler can catch a trout's eye and cause it to stop feeding, or even flee. The right color on a fly can please the trout, causing it to accept an artificial with the kind of satisfaction that results in a hook lodged firmly in the corner of its jaw.

Light Intensity

Trout eyes are able to take in more light than ours. Trout are therefore able to see better in low light than we are. Perhaps that explains why, as evening approaches and it seems it should get easier to fool trout, it sometimes gets harder. They can still see our flies just as well, but we cannot.

Trout begin to adjust from color to black and white vision in late afternoon, four to five hours before dark. During this switch they are not as able to distinguish colors; the color of your fly is less important at dawn and dusk, most important at midday. At twilight and after dark they see only in black and white, making the size and silhouette of a fly the only important factors. In the morning the reverse adjustment occurs over a period of about five hours, and trout are able to distinguish colors again by early to midmorning.

Trout can see to feed anytime their prey is active. They feel more secure feeding in low light and will romp at night if anything is around to eat. Very large fish, especially browns that have reached such size that they become cannibals, move out to feed almost exclusively at night.

Trout have no eyelids. Their eyes can shut out some intense light, but they often avoid bright light by moving into shade or deeper water. That is the main reason you find schools of trout holed up in shadows on sunny days. It is also one of the reasons that trout feed more actively, and closer to the surface, on overcast days.

Underwater Sight

Trout see under the water much as we see in the air. They do not see to the distances we do because water is a denser medium and light rays do not travel as far. But the rays do travel in a straight line, and there is little distortion in calm water.

Lateral visibility depends on the amount of light available. In clear water, at midday, trout see as far as fifty to seventy-five feet. Cloudy water reduces lateral vision to as little as four or five feet. Under most conditions, however, it can be assumed that trout see quite well at ranges from five to twenty feet. The rougher the water, the more distorted any object will appear within that range. That is why you are able to approach trout almost to rod-tip distances in tumbling pocket water.

One bit of trout behavior is impossible for me to explain, and I have not seen any explanation for it in anything I've read. But it has been observed over and over, and you have probably noticed it, too. Trout are not spooked by the submerged legs of a wading angler in deep water, the dangling appendages of a float tuber in still water, or the close but quiet approach of a skin diver along the bottom. If you move fast they bolt. But they don't seem to be disturbed unless the movement is abrupt and becomes threatening.

Perhaps that is the answer: trout are not spooked because they don't feel threatened by our legs under the water. It certainly works to our advantage. How many times have you waded a three- to four-foot-deep run, fished it with a weighted nymph, and taken trout not far from your feet? It happens all the time. Trout down there have to see our legs; they must be aware of them, must know they are foreign objects. Yet they continue to feed.

I won't try to explain it, but will tell you how to take advantage of it: when fishing close, don't move fast when you wade between casts, and don't wade while you fish out a cast. Keep your looming figure as unthreatening as you can, and you'll take fish you shouldn't be able to take according to what we know about the underwater vision of trout.

The Trout's Window

Light rays have mass. They travel through air in a straight line until they meet a denser medium. Then they are refracted, which means they are bent. The image of any object carried on them is sent in the new direction with them. Water is a denser medium. When light rays strike the surface and enter the water, they are refracted at an angle of 48½ degrees. Light passing back out of water into the air is bent at the same angle.

The lowest angle a light ray can carry a distinct image through the water's surface is 10 degrees. Below that angle light rays are reflected; they bounce off, but not like rubber balls off pavement. A few rays still get through, sometimes enough to carry a faint

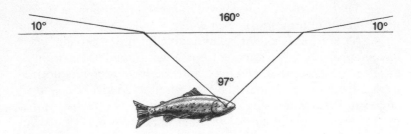

Trout have a window on the outside world that covers a 160-degree arc, but it is compressed into a 97-degree arc under the water because of the angle of refraction as light rays pass through the surface of the water.

image. But most rays are reflected off the surface and back into the air. Trout can't see much of what goes on in that 10-degree angle immediately above the surface.

The arc of vision above the surface is compressed by refraction and delivered to the trout's eye. It becomes the trout's cone of vision. The top of the cone is the trout's circular window out to the world above the water. The window travels with the trout wherever it goes, constantly opening up new views above. As the trout moves closer to the surface, the size of the window diminishes. As it moves deeper, the window opens up, growing larger in proportion to the depth.

An object straight overhead, above the trout, is perfectly clear because those light rays strike the surface at a 90-degree angle; they are not bent. As an object moves toward the periphery of the window, its light rays are bent more, compressed more, and the object's image becomes increasingly distorted.

The entire visible world above a trout is seen through its window: the land surface in sight becomes a circle of visible objects surrounding the sky straight overhead. Anything above the trout's horizon will project inward, into the window. If the surface of the water is smooth, as on a glassy flat, and you step out onto the bank, suddenly looming into a trout's window, every move you make is starkly visible, etched against the sky.

It's time to put some of this optical stuff into practical terms, things that determine what you can do out there on the stream without alarming the trout you'd like to catch.

Because of its circular window, the trout's view of the world above water is shaped like a circle, with objects on the periphery of it projecting into the circle.

That 10-degree angle of reflection, for example, defines how close you can approach a trout without looming into its window. If a trout holds two feet deep, and you approach it from the bank, then at various distances you must assume certain postures to stay below the trout's line of sight. At about ten feet, its line of sight is approximately a foot above the surface, and to keep out of sight you would have to crawl on your belly. At twenty feet the line of sight is about three feet above the surface, and to keep out of sight you should be on your knees. At thirty feet, which is probably the range at which a trout's vision begins to be at least a little distorted by distance, the line of sight is five feet above the surface, and you should kneel or stoop. At forty feet, clearance leaps up to seven feet, and there are few of us who couldn't stand straight up and still be out of sight of the trout.

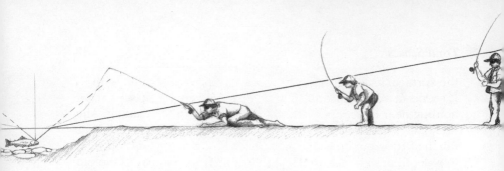

To stay completely out of a trout's window, below its 10-degree line of sight, you must lower your profile as you get closer. Sometimes it's not necessary, because of distance and distortion, but it's wise to keep it in mind.

If you keep yourself out of sight, don't fail to do what you can to keep your rod out of sight as well. Simply tip it over and make your false casts with the rod parallel to the water. Keep this in mind any time you stalk trout within forty feet. The closer you get, the more you should tilt the casting plane.

The same figures apply when you wade, but you get to subtract that portion of yourself that is below your own waterline. That is not to say that at ten feet you would have to wade up to your neck. But it does say you cannot get much closer than fifteen feet while wading waist deep, because that is where you have two and a half feet of clearance below the trout's line of sight. At twenty-five feet you have four feet of clearance, which is about the point at which you should begin to worry about getting yourself into the trout's view, unless you are wading in very shallow water or you are extraordinarily tall.

As a trout moves up in the water column, say to within a foot of

It seems at first glance that when a trout rises in the water column, its window shrinks, and you can move right up on it. But it's not so easy: the 10-degree angle of reflection remains the same and is parallel to the old one, so that you can only step forward five feet or so without getting into the reduced window.

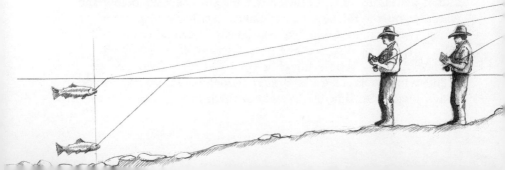

the surface, its window shrinks, and its line of sight lifts with it. It seems at a casual glance that you can move right up on a trout holding near the surface. But that first glance is misleading. The line of sight does rise with the trout, but it doesn't rise nearly as much as the trout does. If a trout moves from a depth of four feet to a depth of one foot, the new line of sight is parallel to the old line of sight, and just above it. The rise in the line of sight is less than a foot.

It seems that you could gallop right up to a fish feeding a few inches under the surface. The truth is that this near-surface feeding decreases the distance to which you can approach the trout without getting caught in its window by about five feet. That's all.

The factor of focus alters all of this to a certain extent. The shallower a trout holds, the nearer its focus becomes on whatever it is feeding. The nearer its focus, the more objects on the periphery of its window are out of focus. But a trout's eye reaches infinite focus at only two feet: if it concentrates on something at two feet, everything beyond the object of its attention is also in focus. That means a trout has to hold very high in the water, only a few inches to a foot deep, and focus intently on something very near it, before you can enter its window and be out of its focus. And if you suddenly wave something about, for instance a fly rod, the trout can change its focus in an instant, bringing you alarmingly into its view.

All of the rules of trout vision are subject to the amount of distortion of the water itself. Light penetrates easily through the surface of flat water. It does not do so well through the tossed water of a riffle or run. Instead of a threat looming over a trout, you become an unsteady outline in what has been called a kaleidoscope of pictures, all of them in constant motion.

That does not mean that you can run right up to a riffle and take fish at your feet. It does mean that with a careful approach, and a minimum of fast movement both above and below the water, you can work a lot closer to your fish in rough water.

The Mirror

The window is a circle through which trout see the world above water. Outside of that circle all light rays are reflected away from the water, and these reflected rays bring no message to the eyes of trout.

The same thing happens beneath the surface. Outside the window, rays of light are reflected back into the eye of the trout. The entire surface of the water surrounding the window becomes a mirror reflecting whatever is underneath it.

A drifting insect or a submerged artificial appears to the trout twice: once in its actual position, and once again reflected from the surface. This is excellent information; it might double the chance that a trout sees our fly. But it doesn't have much effect on the way we fish sunken flies. The mirror does have an effect when we fish drys, because it changes the way a trout perceives a dry fly as it arrives on a current.

When a dry fly sits in the trout's window, the trout sees it in a direct line of sight. Its features—tail, body, hackle, and wings—appear as they might to us, with the exception of some distortion where the fly touches the water. That is the way we envision a trout perceiving a dry fly, no matter where it sits on the water. But what happens when that same fly sits outside the window?

The only thing a trout would see of an insect or artificial fly sitting on the surface outside of its window is a few points of light where hackle and tail bend the surface film, dimpling the mirror. The trout does not see any portion of the fly itself unless part of it penetrates the surface film and hangs down into the trout's underwater world.

As a dry fly floats toward a trout, the trout's first impression, then, is of those starlike bursts of light. If you fish fast water—a riffle or rough run—that might be the trout's only impression,

Outside the 97-degree cone of vision that is the trout's window on the world, all light rays are reflected back off the underside of the surface, and it becomes a mirror reflecting objects underwater.

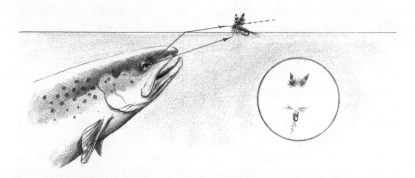

When a natural or an imitation approaches the trout's window it looks disembodied, as seen in the inset. The wings are seen in the window; the hook and everything underwater is seen directly. When the fly enters the window the disembodied parts merge.

and it might be enough to draw the trout to the surface for a strike.

If the water is slick on top, though, the points of light should conform, at least to a certain extent, to what the trout has been seeing as it feeds. If they do, the trout's interest will be aroused, and it will begin to rise to examine the fly. If the fly looks satisfactory as it enters the window, then the trout will complete the rise to take it. But how does the fly appear as it enters the window? It appears disembodied.

Due to that 10-degree angle of reflection, the tip of the wings, which poke up highest, will enter the window first, almost as if standing on their toes to peek over the edge of it. The wings will be separate from the rest of the fly, which is still approaching the window and just a few points of light in the mirror. As the fly gets closer to the window the wings emerge into view, and they begin to merge with those points of light.

When the fly enters the window, the wings and body merge at the same time the body of the fly becomes visible to the fish. Most fish have made up their minds by this time, and either accept the fly or reject it. But there are finicky feeders, almost always brown trout on smooth water, that continue to inspect the fly, following it downstream, nose almost to hackle tips. What are they doing?

In their excellent book *The Trout and the Fly* (Nick Lyons Books, 1980), British authors Brian Clarke and John Goddard suggest these fish are examining the fly in what is known as Snell's Circle. This is a band of iridescent light surrounding the edge of the window in which all of the colors of an insect or fly pattern show up most clearly. Goddard and Clarke speculate that fish displaying what has been termed a *complex rise* hold the fly in the precise area of their moving window where they can examine it most precisely, and at leisure. I have had it happen to me only often enough to know that it is unnerving. Trout rarely take at the end of such critical scrutiny.

The wings of a mayfly dun are its most salient feature. When you select an imitation and present it to selective fish on smooth currents, it should be a winged imitation because the wing is what a trout sees first as the fly approaches the window. If hackles are used, they should be the color of the wing, not the legs of the insect. This is because hackles will show up above the surface as a haze around the wing long before they will show up in the window itself. If a trout can perceive colors perfectly when an insect or its imitation passes through the rim of the window, through Snell's Circle, then it becomes important to match the colors of the natural's body and wings as closely as you can.

Mayfly spinners and many terrestrial insects lie awash in the surface film. Their bodies penetrate the surface film, and a trout is able to see not only their color but also their shape before they enter the window. When fishing glassy water with spinner or terrestrial imitations, it is best to have everything as close to the natural as you can get it.

The window and mirror are factors mainly when fishing smooth water, which is why imitation of the size, form, and color of a natural is far more important on flats than it is on riffles and runs. Where the water is rough, it is wiser to concentrate on those points of light and show the fish a fly that floats well, dancing on the surface with a certain air of enticement.

HEARING

Fish have no outer ears, as we do. For centuries there was great debate between those who thought trout had hearing, and those who thought they did not. But science eventually resolved the question through experimental evidence that proved fish react to sounds, and then through dissection that revealed trout have inner ears surprisingly like our own.

Water is an excellent conductor of sound waves, better than air. A fish has no outer ears because it is already suspended in the medium through which the sound waves travel. The information impinges directly on the skull and is transmitted to the inner ear.

In addition to their inner ears, trout sense low-frequency sounds through their lateral lines. To get an idea how this might work, strike a note on a piano while you have your other hand spread flat on the instrument; you will *feel* the sound. Trout are equipped to pick up noises such as footfalls above a cutbank or the knocking together of stones while you wade.

Hearing in all but peaceful water is masked to a certain extent by constant noise that already exists in the world of the trout. We hear the rushing sound of a riffle as it rapidly bounds down its course. It must be comparably loud to a trout, causing a confusion of sounds from which it might be difficult to sort out those that are threatening. It is another reason trout can be approached closer in tumbling water.

Sounds transmitted through air do not penetrate into water, at least to the extent that trout can hear them. In an early experiment reported in his *The Fly-Fisher's Entomology,* Alfred Ronalds observed a trout holding in six inches of water while a shotgun was held out of sight and fired near the trout. It had no effect. Trout do not eavesdrop on anglers' conversations. You can even shout.

Trout easily pick up the sounds of clumsy wading, thuds on the bottom of a boat, or the rattle and creaking of oars. Any sort of noise that might be transmitted through water should be kept to a minimum.

LATERAL LINE

A sense organ, the lateral line is found only in fish. It is essentially a tube running just beneath the skin and scales of the trout, on both sides, from the tail to the gill covers. It contains a nerve trunk that sends out branches at intervals. These penetrate the skin and scales through pores and have sensory nerve endings. The lateral line gathers information from the water and seems to serve at least three functions for the fish.

The first function of the lateral line is to pick up very low-frequency vibrations, lower than man or fish can hear. So in this sense it is a hearing organ, used to pick up a cautious footstep or the straining of an oar against an oarlock.

The lateral line's second function is to serve as a long-distance touch organ. This is an extension of the sound sense. A trout might feel the vibrations, and thus sense the approach of an otter entering the water and swimming toward it. A trout might feel the vibrations of the passage of another trout. It might even perceive the excited movements of the other trout as it pounces on a stonefly nymph. A trout holding in placid water would feel the vibrations of other trout making splashy rises near its lie. The lateral line is part of the reason most trout in a pool seem to respond at the same time when a hatch of mayfly duns or caddis adults begins to make things exciting. The lateral line picks up the news.

The third function of the lateral line is to warn trout about abrupt changes in water temperature. Because they are cold-blooded, trout are not aware of heat and cold in the same sense that we are. It takes time for their metabolisms to respond to changes in temperature. Sudden changes cause problems in their inner workings, which is why trout can adjust to stressful temperatures that come on slowly, but die if the change is abrupt. The lateral line warns a trout of such a change and drives it to seek water closer to the temperature of the water in which it has been holding.

The lateral line might serve other purposes about which scientists are not yet aware. Its main function, however, is to supply that combination of low-frequency hearing and long-distance touching related to vibrations in the water. Again, it's a warning to you not to make those vibrations.

SMELL AND TASTE

The sense of smell is closely intertwined with the sense of taste. Both are ways of sampling whatever is in the water, and both give some report on what is good for the trout and what is bad for it.

Its sense of smell samples traces of chemicals at a distance and allows the trout to get a sense about something without being in touch with it. This sense is alarmingly acute; in experiments, small amounts of bear, seal, or human scent have driven fish away from a fish ladder. It has been speculated that an angler wearing waders will alarm far fewer trout than one wading wet. It is worth considering.

A trout tastes things only when it touches them. Taste buds are located on the tongue and in the mouth. There is little doubt our imitations taste terrible compared to the real thing, which is why when a trout takes a fly in, you've got to set the hook quickly before it spits the fly back out.

The tactile sense comes into play at the same time. An artificial fly no doubt feels like a fake the instant it is taken. This would be especially true for flies constructed with bodies of hard synthetic materials, or with tails and feelers that are stiff and sharp. It is the reason behind much of traditionalist thinking in fly tying: furs and other soft body materials, and pliable fibers such as hackle or flank, will not fool a fish for long, but might induce it to hang onto a fly for a few extra seconds, during which the hook can be successfully set.

This discussion of the senses of trout has been dominated by sight. It might not seem fair, but I have seen a drawing of a trout's brain compared to that of a shark and a dog. Sharks find their prey by smell; the olfactory regions of their brains are large, the optical lobes tiny. A dog does a bit of thinking when gathering its meals and going about its other concerns; a dog's cerebral hemispheres loom large above small optical lobes.

A trout's brain, which is not much bigger than a pea, is dominated by its optical lobes. Sight is most important to a trout, both in its defenses and in its feeding. Sight is therefore most important to the angler who hopes to be a successful predator of trout.

The trout's cerebral equipment is minute, which makes you wonder how it manages to outwit us so often.

PART II
Trout Tactics

3

Levels of the Game

You can wade into fly fishing as deep as you want. The game has all sorts of levels. Each of the levels has its own puzzles, and its own rewards for solving the puzzles.

It is a thrill for an experienced angler to stalk into position above a trout rising selectively to something so small it is almost invisible, to drop a tiny next-to-nothing precisely on the trout's nose and in time for its next rise, and to see the trout rise confidently to the take and turn back down. It is rewarding to see the trout thrash in surprise when it feels the bite of that minute barb.

It is just as much a thrill for the beginner to master the basic cast for the first time, to read the water and divine a prospective lie, to place a big, searching dry in what looks like the right spot with a thirty-foot cast, and to see an eager trout spear up to take with an approving swirl. Maybe this is more thrilling; the pleasure of this kind of fishing draws the most experienced fly fisherman back time after time, long after he has mastered a few of what are considered the higher levels of the game.

LEVELS OF EXPERTISE

Everybody is a beginner. There are no levels in fly fishing for trout at which there's not a lot left to learn. The more experienced a person becomes, then the broader the fronts across which he tries to push his knowledge and abilities: about flies, hatches, tackle, casting, and all other aspects of the sport. That is what propels a person toward expertise.

A novice might feel he faces the most difficult moments in the sport – learning to cast a fly and catch those first few trout. Actually he has it easiest. He has only to select the right tackle, then to master the basic cast and a few casts built around it. It can be done in a few hours, a few days, or a few weeks.

The earliest steps are most rewarding. Progress is made in lightninglike bounds, and doors are opened everywhere you turn. There are lots of books to read, videos to view, and trout streams to fish for the first time with an open mind. If you are a beginner you have a command to fish a lot, for only by fishing can you interpret what you've learned into what really works to take trout out on streams.

You can learn a lot from those who have fished more than you have, or who have fished a certain water type or method and learned more about it than you might know. If I had a single bit of brilliant advice to offer, in order to raise your level of expertise, it would be to fish with folks who are more experienced than you are. Watch what they do and ask them dumb questions.

But the trout is the best teacher. And you'll learn most from trout on a home river.

Everybody is an expert on his home waters. A novice can take a more experienced fisherman out and dazzle him, at times, by fishing waters he's fished a few times. He knows where the fish lie, when they feed, what flies they take, what presentations work best.

Home waters offer other advantages. They are likely small and sprinkled with all the various water types you've eventually got to learn to fish: riffles, runs, pools, flats, and banks. Concentrate on the bumpier water at first; it forgives even flawed presentations. As your skills improve, look for tougher trout, in smoother currents.

It is one of the curiosities of our sport that in the end we chase the Holy Grail, the toughest fishing: selective trout. But don't make this mistake too soon. We've all read about the meccas of fly fishing – the Beaverkill and Letort in the East, the Bighorn and Henry's Fork of the Snake in the West. These fabled waters hold lots of trout. They are also fished by lots of trouters. Their fish are educated by the frequent stings of sharp hooks, selective to hatches that are often overabundant, and wary because of the exposed waters in which they live and feed. Meccas are not easy to fish, though they do, as promised, provide the best – the most challenging – trout fishing when you're ready for it.

Go to the meccas if you must, but expect to be humbled there at first. I go to them, still expect to be humbled by them, and get my expectations fulfilled at least a few times on every trip. I do better, and you'll do better, on home waters. They are where you learn the most, at least in the beginning.

LEVELS AT WHICH TROUT FEED

Where trout hold and feed in the water column depends on the presence, absence, and activity of the creatures they eat. If food is occasional and varied, trout take stations at holding lies along the bottom and feed opportunistically, moving to at least examine most of what passes by. If food is concentrated, and of a single variety, they will move onto feeding lies, most often still along the bottom, at times at mid-depths, at rarer times a few inches from the surface. But trout always hold in the best position to intercept whatever food is available.

Trout often feed on top, visibly, but they don't always hold there. It's a vulnerable position, exposed to predation from overhead. A heavy hatch will bring them up, sometimes causing them to suspend just a few inches below the surface, but they are wary when they do. The reasons are obvious. Just the other day, during a Pale Morning Dun hatch on the Bighorn River in Montana, I watched an osprey flap overhead with a fine, fat brown trout clutched in its talons: a trout that held too high in the water and was not wary enough.

When trout feed on the surface it's an obvious indication to fish dry flies. Searching dressings, visible and bold, are the best dry flies to use when trout hold on the bottom but rush to the top for a take. More imitative patterns become necessary when trout hold high in the water column and feed selectively on a specific hatch.

Trout feed just subsurface whenever a stage of the hatching insect is vulnerable before it reaches the surface film, or even as it tries to penetrate the film itself. Trout also feed just beneath the surface when a windfall of terrestrials or a mayfly spinner fall puts a lot of insects on the water, sucks them under, and washes them down with the current.

Subsurface trout are often given away by visible rises. They turn with each take, and a boil breaks upward that resembles a rise ring. It is often difficult to tell them from actual surface rises. One way to tell is to look for bubbles that usually accompany a true surface rise. If the bubbles are missing, the take is usually subsurface. Another way is to watch floating insects—duns, caddis adults, midges, or whatever—and see if they go down in rises. If none do, suspect subsurface feeding and switch to emerger patterns or to wet flies fished shallow.

It is rare to find fish feeding at mid-depths. Most trout food found at this level is on its way somewhere else. Most insects in the middle of the water column are bound from the bottom to the top for emergence. When lots of insects begin to make the transition, however, trout will follow them and feed on them at mid-depths. It is territory best explored with a wet fly on the swing, or a weighted nymph fished on a cast that is made slightly upstream and fished out downstream, with the fly a foot or two deep. But most fishing done at mid-depths is a simple failure to reach the bottom.

The bottom is where trout feed most of the time, where they take 80 to 90 percent of their food. It is where they live when they are on holding lies, on prime lies, and on lots of feeding lies as well. The bottom is where a trout leaves the starting blocks when it begins its dash to the top to take a dry fly drifting overhead on bouncy water. A fish that scoots up for a dry can be caught down below on a nymph just as well, though perhaps with more effort and less visible splash and dance for reward.

But there are more times when trout hold on the bottom and are reluctant to move far from it. You need to learn to fish for them where they spend most of their time and do most of their feeding.

LEVELS OF IMITATION

There are three levels of imitation: *suggestive, impressionistic,* and *imitative*. They are different ways to inform the trout of the same thing—here is something good to eat. Each of the three levels is based on the same aspects of the natural: its size, form, and color, in my opinion in that order of importance.

Suggestive dressings are just that: rough suggestions of the kinds of foods that trout eat most often. These foods vary from stream to stream, but certain dressings represent a lot of what trout eat on all streams. Examples are the Royal Wulff and Humpy drys, Gold-Ribbed Hare's Ear and Zug Bug nymphs, and the Woolly Bugger series of streamers. Most of these resemble more than one type of food. The Hare's Ear nymph, as an example, looks a little like a caddis worm, a mayfly or stonefly nymph, a cranefly larva, or even a scud. Whenever you fish a suggestive pattern, you wave in front of the trout's nose a suggestion of many things it might have recently eaten.

Such nonspecific patterns are best used when trout are not feeding visibly, and they are the best kind of flies to use then. They are excellent choices for what I call *searching situations,* when you want to explore the water because fish are not active, and nothing hatches to tell you what fly pattern might work best to goad them into action. Choose the level at which you want to

Suggestive, impressionistic, and imitative styles of dry flies (left to right): Royal Wulff, traditional Blue-winged Olive, and Little Olive Comparadun.

fish – top, subsurface, mid-depths, or bottom – and use an appropriate suggestive dressing to fish it.

Impressionistic dressings capture a few more of the features of a natural insect. An impressionistic dressing should be chosen based on the size, form, and color of something the trout seem to be taking most often. You might determine this by observing what you sweep out of the air in your hat, by lifting rocks out of the water and watching what scurries around on their undersides, or by examining the stomach contents of a fish to see what it has been eating.

An impressionistic dressing is a closer copy of a specific order of insects, but usually represents a number of species within the order. For example, the Adams resembles a wide variety of grayish mayfly duns, the Elk Hair Caddis is quite like dozens of tannish caddis adults, and the Pheasant Tail nymph could be taken for many species of Little Olive nymphs or caddis larvae or midge pupae. A Muddler Minnow is an impressionistic dressing for all of the sculpin family of fishes, and suggests a lot of other things.

Impressionistic dressings are most useful when a food type dominates the fishing scene, but is not being taken selectively. You could likely take a few trout on a suggestive Humpy when most of what they are taking are caddis, but you might do much better with an impressionistic Elk Hair Caddis.

Imitative patterns are best left for those few occasions when they are truly needed. The need will be dictated by a combination of two conditions: selective feeding and smooth waters. When trout feed on one stage of one species, and are able to get a good look at the natural or its imitation, an impressionistic pattern might not be close enough to fool trout. The *form* of the dressing must change, in order to show the trout an unhindered silhouette based on the natural. But the size must be right or you'll find yourself fishless, and the color, if not exact, will not suffer from being a close copy of the real thing.

LEVELS OF FINESSE

I will say that there are two levels of finesse, though it's an oversimplification. I know I am full of beans when I divide so

sharply something that is a continuum from brutally smashing a
fly onto the water to laying it on the surface so gently that the fly
itself looks around to see how it got there. The division helps to
define things though, and to set some goals, so it might be worth
laying out even if it is slightly wrong. Here it is: there is *searching
fishing*, or fishing the water, and *imitative fishing*, or fishing the
hatches.

Searching fishing is what we do during nonfeeding periods, or
at least during periods when fish do not rise and feed visibly and
selectively. The water fished this way is usually wrinkled – a
riffle or run. The flies cast, whether drys, wets, nymphs, or
streamers, are usually larger and more roughly tied than those
fished as imitations of a specific hatch. Searching fishing is the
province of suggestive and impressionistic dressings. Tackle can
be somewhat stouter, more bossy, than that used when fishing
smaller and more delicate dressings.

Imitative fishing is obviously pursued during feeding periods.
Trout might move selectively to a specific nymph, larva, or pupa
under water. They might rise fussily to a single mayfly dun or
spinner, a specific caddis or stonefly adult. When trout feed with
narrow interests you've got to show them something close to
what they're taking, in a way that gets it to them the same way
the natural arrives. It usually takes delicate tackle to do it right.

PRESENTATION VERSUS IMITATION

I recently read a book on dry-fly fishing that was excellent, but
I judged it a little too harsh on entomology and imitation. The
author is a strict presentationist and hinted that imitation is an
affectation. His theories are right for him, but wrong for many
of us.

There are some fly fishermen to whom imitation *is* an affectation, and other anglers who take entomology too far, neglecting
all other factors of fly fishing, feeling they can solve all problems
if only they can identify an insect species and create the perfect
imitation for it. They are wrong, too. It takes a balance between
presentation and imitation.

The argument about presentation versus imitation is ancient,
and academic. Placing one above the other is wrong. Only as

both begin to approach reality do trout begin to applaud. Reality differs from riffle to run to pool to flat, but the fly must look alive and be presented to the fish in a lifelike manner before trout will pay it more than a boil of attention. For those who haven't learned it yet, a boil under the fly is a rejection.

The argument between presentation and imitation was put to rest concisely in another recent work, and I would like to quote the work and recommend it here. Datus Proper, in *What the Trout Said*, wrote, "Presentation is part of imitation, not something opposed to it." They are parts of the same thing.

THE GOAL OF THE GAME

The goal of tactics is the same whether you fish the water or fish over hatches. It is the same whether you fish over lies you suspect might hold trout, or cast to fish you can watch as they feed. The goal is identical whether you fish the top, subsurface, mid-depths, or bottom, and the same no matter which fly type you fish: drys, wets, nymphs, or streamers. *The goal of tactics is to move into position so the trout, visible or suspected, is unaware of your presence as a threat to it, and then to present your fly so the trout is not aware that the fly is connected to a line, leader, and you.*

All sorts of factors go into achieving the goal: tackle selection, casting skills, unobtrusive clothes, and stealthy wading movements that don't startle fish, leaders in balance with the flies tied to them, and flies that resemble foods the trout have been eating. It all relates to the senses of trout. You must not alert them through their sensitive hearing. You must keep yourself out of the angle of their sight, and place your fly where it rides the mirror right into their window of vision.

All of these things take practice, and practice sneaks toward perfect more often by stumbling than it does by leaps. Work out the fundamentals of fishing before you take on its most difficult challenges. Build a solid base, until you can execute the basic tactics without pausing to direct each movement of each hand in the cast or drift of the fly.

As Ray Bergman put it in *Trout*, "Once the fundamentals become instinctive you do the necessary things without thought. Then you can elaborate to good advantage."

4

Fishing the Searching Dry

Fly fishing for trout starts with the searching dry fly. It is the easiest method to use on most kinds of moving water, therefore the most effective tactic for the average angler in the average situation.

That statement might startle many modern nymph fishermen, who will, in truth, find their own methods more productive most of the time. But they will have to confess that the fly fisherman who masters the searching dry spends many days stumbling before he can finally and consistently bring trout to the net using a nymph.

American trout streams are so varied that trout living in them see a wide variety of foods floating overhead every day. Given water of modest depth and flow, trout are willing to spear to the top to make the splashy take. That sudden surprise take to the searching dry fly is one of the largest thrills in fly fishing. It is there for the plucking by the neophyte fly fisherman, or by the expert. It is constantly denied those who fish by any other method.

SEARCHING DRY FLIES

Dry flies designed for fishing the water, as opposed to matching hatches, should combine certain elements that make them most useful for the task. The first is *flotation*. They will be cast over a wide variety of water types and must float on the worst of them. Patterns that perch on the tips of their hackles do the best job of riding out difficult water. The points of light caused by all those hackle tips, where they poke the surface film, give the impression of something living when seen from down below.

Searching dressings must also be *visible*. If you can't see a fly, you can't follow its drift. This causes two problems: you won't know when it's fishing the way you want it to, and you won't know when a trout takes it, unless the rise is so obvious that it catches your attention from wherever it might have wandered.

Another element of a good searching dry is the indefinable aspect that gives it the *appearance of life*. All good drys have this; they look like something nature might have created. This aspect is wrapped up in the way the fly is designed: its tails and body, wings and hackles. The impression of life also stems from a resemblance to one of the orders of natural insects. Traditional Catskill drys look alive because they resemble the natural mayfly

Two of the best searching dressings for any water, the Elk Hair Caddis (left) and Royal Wulff.

dun. The Elk Hair Caddis looks alive because it is such an impressionistic rendition of the adult caddisfly.

The final aspect of the good searching dry is one that you must bring to the fly: *confidence.* No fly will work well, even if it floats, is visible, and looks alive, if you don't think it's going to catch fish. Any fly will work well if you are certain it's just about to trick the trout out of their scales, so long as it contains the other three elements. The confidence factor is one good reason to start with some searching drys that have long and brilliant histories: you know they have caught thousands of fish.

Many searching drys resemble lots of different insects, which gives them a better chance to remind a trout about something it has eaten recently. The Adams is an example. It has the standard Catskill shape, and therefore the form of a mayfly dun. Its grayish tones give it roughly the colors of dozens of mayfly species. But the Adams was originally designed to represent a flying caddis, and it also looks a lot like a midge when fished in smaller sizes.

Some of the best dry flies seem to have no connection to any insect whatever. The most commonly cited example is the Royal Coachman. It has white wings and a body that is alternately peacock green and bright red. But this popular fly is not as unnatural as it seems. Its colors darken when wet, and the body becomes a buggy and banded olive/brown/olive. That white wing stands up like a flag, but is obscured from below by the hackle. The wing is perhaps the most valuable feature of the fly; it helps you follow the drift and notice a strike.

The Elk Hair Caddis, Al Troth's successful innovation, is at once an excellent imitative fly and among the best searching flies you can find. It cocks well on the water, rides high, and with its light-colored wing is easy for the fisherman to see. Apparently, trout see it quite well, too, and take it for a wide variety of things. It fishes well whenever caddis are around, which is almost continually after the first warm weeks of the season.

When I want to fish a dry searching pattern, and I see no evidence in the air or on the water that some other dressing might be better, the Elk Hair Caddis is the first fly I reach for, usually in #12 or #14.

The second dressing I reach for is the Beetle Bug, again in #12 or #14. The Beetle Bug is a look-alike to the Royal Wulff, but it produces better for me. It's that confidence factor again.

I fished the Beetle Bug constantly when I was young, tying it with a deer-hair tail, red floss body, white calf-tail wings, and coachman hackle, which in those days, given my budget, was a weepy thing from a barnyard rooster. I switched to the Royal Wulff at about the time I began to upgrade my tying materials and abilities. I caught lots of fish for several years on the Wulff dressing.

One day, just a few years ago, Bob Borden told me about some modifications he had worked on the old Beetle Bug. Bob owns a fly-tying products company. He changed the tail of the Beetle Bug from soft deer hair to stiff moose fibers, dyed some fur fluorescent red for the body, and substituted white calf body hair for the crinkly calf-tail wing. The hackle was the same dark coachman brown. "Try it," Bob told me. "For some reason it brings fish up when they won't take anything else."

Of course I didn't believe it. The Elk Hair Caddis was my dressing to bring fish up when nothing else would. I was stuck on the Elk Hair for searching situations. I even fell into the laziness of believing that if it didn't work, it was an indication that nothing else would work either. Sometimes I would fish it for hours without any action. But Bob's mention of the Beetle Bug was sort of nostalgic. I tied half a dozen and put them away in a fly box.

Not long afterward I was on the Deschutes River. It was a lazy midsummer day. The sun was bright on the broad, bouncy riffles, and a few caddis danced over them. My friends fished nymphs with indicators and split shot, and they took lots of trout. But it appeared to be the kind of day, and the kind of water, where trout would rise to drys. I preferred to take mine that way, so I knotted on an Elk Hair Caddis, dressed it with floatant, and fluffed its fibers.

I fished for quite a while, and was mildly astonished when nothing came to the fly. Halfway through the riffle I stopped fishing and listened to my friends shouting in excitement over another nymph-hooked trout. I decided to give up and switch, to fumble with all the attachments of indicator and split shot. I clipped the Elk Hair from my leader, dropped it into my dry fly box, and noticed those bright-winged Beetle Bugs. I tied one on with relief. It was something else to try before I tried what I knew would work: nymphs.

The new version of the old fly didn't produce results that knocked me over in the current. But it did produce four trout before I'd fished to the head of the riffle. That wasn't bad. In fact, it was favorable compared to what my friends were doing with their deadly nymphs. Every time I hooked a trout I played it in their direction and shouted to make sure they would see it. A trout feels ashamed of itself if you don't boast about it a bit.

Since that day I've used the Beetle Bug consistently as my second searching fly, after trying the Elk Hair Caddis. Sometimes it's my first fly. I catch lots of trout on it, and I have lots of confidence in it.

Most searching fishing is done with flies in the middle of the size range of natural insects, which is the narrow range from #10 down to #14. If there is an average searching dry fly, it would be tied on a #12 hook in the West, where it would tend to be a bushy hairwing fly, and a #14 hook in the East, where it would tend to be a sparse Catskill dressing.

TACKLE FOR FISHING THE WATER

In *Tackle and Technique for Taking Trout,* I recommended thinking about trout outfits in terms of light, medium, and heavy. Tackle for searching drys should be your medium, if you have one. But having said that, I need to amend it. My medium rod is 8½ feet long and casts a 6-weight line. But I am not always so heavily armed when out for a day on a trout stream. Often I expect to fish a hatch sometime during the day, and I am armed for that. I fish the water until the hatch starts; I don't run for the car to switch rods when it happens.

Most of the time I carry an 8-foot 5-weight outfit. It is, at present, my light rod. But it's not by chance that this rod serves well in situations where I want to fish the water, and also in situations where I want to fish the hatches. It's a compromise and works well for both.

The right outfit depends in part on the size streams you fish. I carry a 7-foot 4-weight outfit when fishing tiny water, and almost all of my fishing on tiny water is searching fishing with dry flies. I have read recommendations for long rods on small streams. If I fished my favorite small stream with a 9-foot rod I would break it in the forest before I got to the water. But that longer rod, balanced to a 5- or 6-weight line, would be just right for searching drys on bigger water.

Lines for fishing the water should be whatever floating line you carry on your reel: double-taper, weight-forward, long-belly or triangle-taper. Any will do. If you have a reason to prefer one over the other, that is the best line for you. If it helps, I use a double-taper for the line control it gives me in all situations.

Leaders should be about the length of the rod, a little longer if your water tends to be smoother, but no shorter even if it's rougher. An eight- to ten-foot leader, if properly tapered, will give you all the control you need.

For years I paid no attention to tippets when fishing the water. Somewhere back in my own dark ages I learned that a tippet should be fourteen inches long. I probably read it in a book referring to gut leaders, and it was probably right for gut. So I started each day with a tippet that was too short, and clipped it back with every lost fly until it got down to eight inches or so. The shorter it got the fewer fish I caught. But it took me years to figure out the tippet was the problem.

The leader tippet should start out at about two feet long, and it should be replaced before it gets down to the fourteen or so inches that I used to consider just right. The tippet should also be balanced to the size of the fly: 4X (.007-inch) and 5X (.006-inch) leaders usually turn over well with flies in the typical searching size range — #10 to #14. For larger flies, and larger fish, go up an X or so.

Certain peripheral gear serves searching fishing, though it is one type of fly fishing where you can pare your encumbrances to the essentials. You need a single box of searching drys to start, and some spare tippet material in a couple of sizes. Beyond that you can get by with clippers to nip your knots, floatant to keep your flies on top, a hemostat to remove the fly from the lip of a fish, and a handkerchief to dry the fly before you dress it after distributing the trout in the direction you want it — more often back into the stream than into your creel, I hope.

That's all you need in the way of tackle. It's possible to spend a day astream with what you can carry in the pockets of a fishing shirt.

INDICATIONS FOR THE SEARCHING DRY

The first indication for using the searching dry is no indication at all: nothing going on that leads you to think you should use something else. If fish rise at anything more than a sporadic clip, even if a single trout rises occasionally but always in the same spot, it's best to take a moment and try to figure out specifically what is going on. You might need to match a hatch. Occasional splashy rises in a riffle or run, though, usually indicate trout feeding opportunistically on whatever comes along. They are good prospects for the searching dry.

The next indication is water in which you would reasonably expect trout to rise to the surface. You wouldn't expect trout to rise all the way to the top in a deep pool. They won't often rise to a dry fly when holding on the bottom of a run that is much more than five feet deep.

Searching drys are best when fished on riffles, in runs, over pocket water, and at the shallow heads and tails of pools. They work well along the banks of brisk water, but are not so effective at the edges of smooth flats. It is reasonable to expect trout to take a searching dry in the fast water between the still-life flats of a meadow stream, but you might not do so well with them on the breathless flats themselves.

Weather can be an indication to use the searching dry. Trout focus upward when the weather is warm in spring and fall, usually in the middle part of the day. They also look up when it's cool in the mornings and evenings of hot midsummer days. But they wrap themselves in fur coats and refuse to rise randomly whenever the water is frigid. When the water is high with spring runoff, or after a rain, trout feed along the bottom and seldom can be coaxed to the top.

This doesn't mean trout won't feed on dry flies in the middle of winter if something hatches to move them. They will. But winter hatches, for the most part, happen on waters with stable temperatures – spring creeks and tailwaters – where the water is not as cold as the air. Whenever these hatches come off, trout feed on them. But this is not an indication for using searching drys in

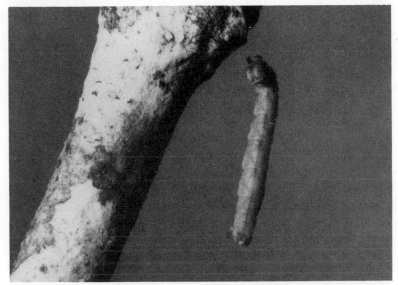

Sporadic insect activity, whether aquatic or terrestrial—such as inch-worms dangling their occasional way into the water—is an indication that fishing the water with searching flies is the best way to go.

winter. When fish feed on a specific hatch at any time of year it is an indication that you should match it, not fish with a searching dry.

Sporadic insect activity, at any time of year, is a better indication that fishing the water will work. The best indication of all is lots of feeding activity on a broad range of insect types. Summer and fall terrestrial time is excellent for flies like the Royal Wulff. Trout sip a few ants, dash for an occasional hopper, find a beetle unhappily awash in the surface film, then take a poke at a caddis dancing above the water. That is the rise you will see, and it gives away a trout that is feeding at random. Drop an Elk Hair Caddis, Beetle Bug, or Royal Wulff over it, and it will likely accept the fly if your presentation is right.

READING WATER

The first step in fishing the water is to determine likely lies, the subject of an earlier book in this series, *Reading the Water*. Trout lies are found in water that offers fish three things: food, a current to deliver it, and shelter that breaks the current so they are not constantly forced to fight it.

Many lies are obvious: the welling of water just above a boulder, or the pocket that forms below it; an indentation along an undercut bank; a plunge pool in a shallow mountain creek. But not all likely lies are pinpoint spots where you find trout surrounded by a vastness of water that holds no trout at all.

Most lies are *areas* of water that look likely: a few feet of riffle, a hundred-foot run, a long current seam alongside choppy water, a broad, dark slick in fast water that indicates a trough or ledge below. These are the kinds of lies you fish when you fish the water.

Most lies fished with searching flies are large areas of holding water that should be covered with a disciplined casting pattern, as opposed to pinpoint lies that are easy to read and cover with just a few casts.

DRAG

Drag is the number-one enemy of the dry-fly fisherman, whether he fishes searching drys or imitations over hatches. Drag is any movement of the fly that is contrary to the movement of the current, or to movements that would be made by an untethered insect adrift on the current.

Naturals sometimes flutter and twitch and hop. But most of the time they drift on the surface patiently and without movement, waiting for the moment they can lift off. Only in rare instances, and usually on lakes, do insects scoot across the surface of the water. Trout know this; a dragging fly causes them to reject it, and may even send the fish scooting themselves.

Drag is caused when the leader is drawn taut by the current. The leader can't move the fly line, which is heavier, so it tugs at the fly, which is lighter. Sometimes you can see drag; the fly leaves a little V-wake behind it. Other times you can't see it. The fly looks as if it is drifting freely, without drag. The float looks good, but it's not always true. If the leader lies on the water straight as an arrow between line tip and fly, then it can exert little unnatural movements that you will never detect.

Drag caused by a straight leader has two solutions. The first is a leader with a tippet long enough and light enough to let the fly land lightly and drift freely. The tippet diameter must be in balance with the fly size in order to turn it over at the end of the cast. If the tippet is too stout it overpowers the fly, delivering it to the water with a splat. The splat itself is bad, but even worse is the straight and stiff leader, which immediately begins waving the fly about.

The second solution is in the cast. Always put just enough punch into it so the leader turns over in the air, *above the water.* When the leader drifts to the water there will be a degree of slack in it. This slack will give the fly some freedom.

The leader is not the only cause for drag. Conflicting currents also cause it. When two or more currents pull in slightly different directions, they manifest themselves by tugging your leader tight when you cast across them. They can't be dealt with by correcting the composition of your leader and tippet. You've got to do it by choosing a casting position that eliminates the need to deal with them. Put yourself into position so that only one current intervenes between you and the lie you want to fish.

You can also deal with conflicting currents by installing some slack into the line and leader when you cast. This is done by wobbling the rod while the line is still in the air: the wiggle cast. The currents will have to remove this slack before the fly drags, and you will get at least a short float.

Drag is damning to the fisher of dry flies. It will defeat you at times without ever exposing itself, especially if you are in the habit of casting forty feet and beyond. There is nothing wrong with fishing at those distances when the water calls for it. There is something wrong with it when you can get closer to your fish, or to the water that you want to explore for fish. The kind of water you fish with searching drys is usually rough enough to distort the vision of holding trout. Use this to your advantage: move in close, where you can see when your fly is dragging, and where you've got some of those conflicting currents behind you rather than between you and your line of drift.

TACTICS FOR THE SEARCHING DRY

Searching is done differently on different type of water. You don't fish a mountain creek the same way you fish an average-sized trout stream. You don't fish a typical trout stream the way you'd approach a big river.

Fishing a small creek with searching drys calls for lots of movement. I'd call it running and gunning, but sometimes I get in such a hurry that I have to slow myself down. I'm too eager to see what's around the next bend; sometimes I trample right over water I ought to fish more carefully. But I've seen more people make the opposite mistake: they stake out a nice stretch of water and fish it until all of the trout have gotten bored and moved to Texas.

Most of the water in a small stream is shallow enough to fish well with searching drys. Trout hold along the bottom, but are usually willing to move to the top. You want to fish all of the water you think might hold fish: plunge pools, boulder pockets in fast water, even flats where the water spreads out and trout tremble along the bottom, waiting for a terrestrial insect to drop out of the trees and into danger.

Trout in small water are apt to see the fly float overhead on the first or second cast. I've seen times when they came to the tenth or even twentieth cast, but these instances are rare. If the fish want the fly at all, most often they boil up as soon as they see it. They are used to making quick decisions, and don't need to be coaxed.

That is why I recommend fishing small streams with lots of movement: it's the best way to show your fly to lots of fish. Fish upstream. Use short casts. Pop your fly onto all of the potential holding water. But fish it with just a few casts. Make sure any trout around has a chance to make a decision. Then move on to the next bit of water.

On trout streams of typical size, you've got to combine movement with patience. The first thing to do is read the water for the kind that looks right for fishing with searching dry flies. Not all of it will be right. For example, some riffles are so shallow—less than about a foot deep—that they aren't likely to hold any trout at all. There is a high percentage of this water on some trout streams, and you save yourself lots of time by eliminating it. Very deep pools are also unlikely water: they hold trout, but will not often send them all the way to the top for a dry unless a hatch draws them into holding higher in the water column.

Typical searching water on trout streams consists of riffles, runs, and pools of moderate depth with some movement to them. You want to move until you find it. When you find it you want to slow down and fish it carefully. Set up a casting pattern so that the fly covers all of the water.

Error number one, when fishing searching drys on medium-sized streams, is getting rooted to one spot, then casting over and over to the same place. It might be the best water, but its potential for producing fish drops the longer you stand there and pound it. Show the fly to some new fish; cover the water thoroughly but not repeatedly. Once you've worn out a riffle or run, move on and find another.

Error number two is moving too fast, fishing an average-sized stream the same quick way you would cover a tiny creek. Move eagerly between bits of holding water. Fish them carefully when you come to them.

Reading water becomes extremely important when you fish big rivers. Potential holding lies are spread out, sometimes with lots of distance between them. When you find them, though, they tend to be spacious, with room for lots of trout. You'll want to fish them patiently, sometimes spending an hour or two in a single riffle or run, especially if it is producing well.

As you walk the banks of a big river, or drift downstream in a boat, watch for water that is shallow enough that trout will come to the top for drys. Make sure it has some current to it; moving water holds more fish, and it's more fun to fish a fly that does something besides fold its arms and sit in one spot. If the water has features—boulders, darkenings that report ledges or trenches, seams where currents come together—then it should be perfect for the searching dry.

When you find water like this, park and fish it for a while. Explore it with your fly.

The Upstream Dry Fly

The primary tactic, when searching the water, is the upstream cast with a dry fly. But the cast should not be made straight upstream unless constraints of the water and landscape require it. Trout point upstream, with their noses into the current; a direct upstream cast shoots the leader and fly, and sometimes even the end of the fly line, right over them. This can cause trout to flee even on rough water.

It is best to get off to one side at an angle, then to cast upstream and across. Nothing soars over the trout on the cast. When a trout moves to take the fly only a slight amount of leader tippet enters its window.

Your position for the upstream dry, then, should be such that you can cast up and at an angle across the current. When fishing a spot lie, such as a plunge pool or piece of pocket water, you should be below it and a few feet to one side. It is best, when fishing such water, to move as close as you can without disturbing trout you suspect might be holding in the water where you want to place the fly. Cast no more than forty to forty-five feet; move closer whenever you can.

When covering an area of holding water, such as a riffle or run, take your position below the closest water you want to fish. Stay back on the bank if the potential holding water creeps right up to

The best position for presenting the upstream searching dry fly is slightly off to the side of the line of current you want to fish.

the edge of the stream. If the water shelves off from shallow to deep, and you don't think trout will be found holding right at the edge, then gauge where you feel the first fish might be as the water deepens, and wade into a position that lets you place your fly onto that water with a cast of modest distance. It pays to look the water over carefully before plunging in; you don't want to wade in water you should be fishing.

It is best to take your position at the downstream end of the fishable water and to wade upstream, if the current is not too strong. You won't send a cloud of silt down ahead of you to warn fish you are coming. If the current is so pushy that you can't wade against it, then it's difficult to fish it with the upstream method. Consider fishing it with cross-stream casts, or even downstream casts, as covered in the next sections.

The cast itself, when fishing the upstream dry, should be the basic overhand fly cast, with no complications. Make the number of forecasts and backcasts that you need to measure the length of the cast and to place it accurately. Aim the delivery stroke about waist high, not directly at the surface. This allows the line and leader to turn over, straighten in the air, and drop lightly to the water. It also allows the leader to waffle a bit, and to land on the water with some slack, which delays drag.

As the fly drifts toward you, gather slack just fast enough to

keep in touch with the fly if a fish takes. In a fast current you've
got to gather slack with long pulls of your line hand. Most of the
time you can draw it in slowly and smoothly, staying just ahead
of the drift of the fly. Don't draw line so fast that you take out all
of the slack, straighten the line and leader, and cause drag. Follow the fly with your rod tip, keep it low, and be ready to set the
hook at any moment.

Don't try for long sweeping drifts on each cast. Five to ten feet
of float are usually plenty, and often about all you are going to get
without unseen drag setting in. Sometimes, especially on riffles,
you can get longer floats, up to fifteen or even twenty feet. But be
cautious of this: a float can look fine to you while not looking fine
at all to the trout. It is best to cover the water with a series of
shorter floats rather than a few that are longer.

Don't be in a hurry to lift the fly off the water at the end of the
float. Let it fish out its drift until drag sets in, or until it has gone
below what you consider potential holding water. Then pick it up
and cast again to a new line of drift a foot or two farther out from
the last one. Fish a series of casts that cover all of the water, each
successive cast covering a line of drift farther away. The first cast
should be nearest your position, and will sometimes be made
straight upstream, or just a few feet out from a line straight
upstream. Each cast after that should cut at a sharper angle
across the stream, placing the fly farther out.

On a small stream, with a narrow lane of holding water, four or
five casts might be all you need to cover what you consider the
worthwhile water in reach. Then you should move up into a new
casting position and repeat the process, covering the next section
of water upstream. There are times, too, when you can stay in
your first position, lengthen your line a few feet, and cover a new
cross section of the holding water without moving. But it is usually best to move upstream and cover it with shorter casts.

When fishing an area of water, as opposed to a specific lie, it is
best to set up some sort of casting pattern to make sure you cover
all of it. Some people imagine a crosshatched grid laid over the
stream. Each square of the grid comprises the area you can cover
with casts from one position. When that water is covered, you
move into a new position that allows you to cover the water in
the next square of the grid. I don't envision streams well in grids

myself, but commend the idea to you if it helps you be sure to cover all of the potential holding water.

Detecting takes to an upstream dry is easy, so long as you keep your eye on the fly. Watch for a splash or bold boil. But you'll be surprised how often your fly disappears in the tiniest pip of a swirl. Whenever you have a hit, set the hook by lifting the rod. It's best to learn a hook set that is a smooth lifting of the rod, rather than an abrupt jerk. The jerk will hook most of the little ones and get them skidding your way. But it will take the fly away from lots of big ones and break off an agonizing share of the others.

The Cross-stream Dry

The upstream dry is the most common way to search the water. But there are places where the tactic doesn't work very well. One is where the current is so pushy that you can't wade against it. It's simply too difficult to get into position to cast upstream. The cross-stream dry can help you then, because you can wade into position at the head of the water to be fished, cover a cross section of it, then move *downstream* into a new casting position.

The cross-stream dry is also useful on a broad width of holding water that is deeper than you want to wade. A cast straight out, rather than to an angle upstream, allows you to cover a wider sweep of water without getting far from the bank.

Your initial casting position should be straight across from the water you want to fish. If wading downstream, you should start at the head of the holding water and fish down. If wading upstream, start at the lower end of it and fish up, just as you did when you waded into position to fish the upstream dry.

The first cast should be made just a few feet upstream from straight across. The object is to get a five- to ten-foot float that is right in front of your position. The cast should cross the stream at such an angle that the first half of the float is above you and the last half of the float is below you.

The initial cast should be made to the near edge of holding water. This will usually be just fifteen to twenty feet out. Each successive cast should be made a foot or two farther out. The

The reach cast helps you get a good drift when presenting a dry fly with a cross-stream cast.

amount of water you can cover this way depends on how far you can see your fly. If it's a tossed riffle, you might have to limit yourself to forty-foot casts. If the water is fairly smooth and you have a clear backcast area behind you, it might be possible to cast fifty-five to sixty feet and still fish your fly well.

Once you have covered all the water you can from the initial position, then move either upstream or downstream into a new position. Draw in all of your line and begin covering the near water with short casts again. Extend the line a foot or two on following casts, sending the fly down a new line of drift. Again, continue casting across stream until you've reached the limit of your ability to follow the drift of the fly, or your ability to cast the fly and get a good drift.

A few line-control tricks help you get good drifts on the cross-stream cast. The first is simply to mend the line whenever a downstream belly begins to form in it, dragging the fly. Roll your rod outward and upward, in a sweeping arc, to lift the downstream belly off the water and toss it over into an upstream belly.

This will give a few extra feet of drag-free drift. It works best on a short cast; the mend is far more difficult to execute on a long cast.

A second technique that helps you fish a drag-free float over conflicting currents is the wiggle cast. As your line shoots out on the delivery stroke, wobble your rod briskly back and forth. The line and leader land on the water in a series of S-curves. The consequent slack allows your fly a long free drift.

One of the best methods for fishing cross-stream calls for the reach cast. It is normally used on smooth water for fine presentations over fussy fish. But it also works well over a riffle or run when currents make it hard to get a good float. The cast is easy to make: just tip the rod over in the upstream direction, parallel to the water, after applying the power for the delivery stroke. The line will come off the rod tip straight to the fly, but the rod tip will be extended a few feet upstream. By following the drift of the fly with the rod you extend the drift of the fly.

It is not difficult to detect takes when using the cross-stream dry. But the longer the cast the harder it is to set the hook. If the cast is long you've got to send the hook-setting message of the lifting rod a long way. Set the hook abruptly, even if the fish is a big one and takes slowly, because all that line and leader act as a shock absorber.

The Downstream Dry

The downstream dry fly gives you an advantage in two situations. The first is in water that you can't wade upstream because the current is too heavy. By turning and wading downstream, fishing ahead of you as you go, you can cover the water well and not wear yourself out. But you can put yourself in danger. It's often best to fish this kind of water by staying back at the edge of it and using the cross-stream cast. I usually restrict the downstream dry in fast water to pockets or short shelves of holding water that I can't reach from any other direction.

The second kind of water for the downstream searching dry is a riffle or run that is fished fairly heavily. Trout in such lies hold on the bottom and are willing to come to the surface for a dry. But they've seen lots of clumsy presentations and have learned to reject a fly if the line and leader go over its head first. The

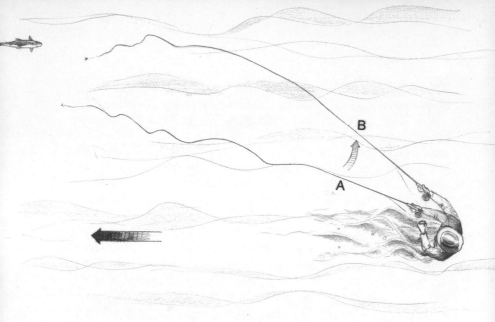

When fishing the dry fly downstream, stop your rod while the line is still in the air (position A); draw it back and tip it over to the side (position B) so the line lands on the water with lots of slack out near the fly.

downstream dry can be effective in such situations because it delivers the fly ahead of line and leader.

Positioning for the downstream dry calls for wading in at the upper end of the water you want to fish. Stay back at the edge, at least at first, and don't wade in water you should be fishing.

The cast should be made at an angle across and downstream. It should be short, say in the twenty- to forty-foot range. You've got to have lots of control over the line before it lands on the water. The reason is obvious: you've got to make some arrangement to let the fly drift downstream without drag. It's easy, but you can't do it with the basic fly cast.

The wiggle cast works well for the downstream dry, but it is best used on slick-water situations, which are usually selective situations, discussed in the next chapter. The best cast for fast water is a created cast, combining elements of the parachute, reach, and wiggle casts. It sounds hard, but it's not. It does, however, require some rod and line control, and some practice.

I like Art Lee's name for this cast. In *Fishing Dry Flies for Trout on Rivers and Streams*, he calls it the *stop and drop*, and I think that describes it almost perfectly. You start with the basic cast, working out the right length of line plus a few extra feet. Assuming you are casting downstream and slightly across, measure the cast beyond where you want the fly to land. Once you've worked out the right amount of line, you are ready for the delivery stroke.

The delivery stroke is made by making a standard forward cast. After the power is put into the cast, and the line is almost straight in the air above the water, abruptly stop the rod. This causes the line to recoil slightly, forming a series of curves — slack — in it. Let it drop to the water that way, and you have the stop and drop. Hold your rod upright. As soon as the fly lands it will start drifting downstream ahead of line and leader. When the slack inserted by the stop is taken out, you can lower your rod and extend the free drift. You should have no problem getting five to ten feet of good float this way.

I have developed some wrinkles in my own casting to improve this tactic. First, I execute the normal basic cast and stop the rod abruptly, as in the stop and drop. But then I tip the rod over, into a partial reach cast, and sometimes wiggle it at the same time. It might sound like a lot to be doing at once, but after you've worked out the basic casting stroke these modifications to it are easy to add.

The wiggle cast, especially if combined with some slight elements of the reach cast, can give your dry fly a long drift on a downstream cast.

This combination of reach and wiggle increases the amount of free float you can get out of each drift. This is important when fishing downstream because every pickup disturbs the water at the end of the drift. If you work a cross section of riffle or run, placing each cast a foot or two outside the line of drift of the cast before it, then the water across the bottom of that cross section will have been disturbed. If you can get a ten- or even fifteen-foot drift, you cover a higher percentage of water than you disturb. It makes a difference.

When you have covered the water you can reach from the initial casting position, then drop down to a new position that lets you cover another cross section of water below the water where you've lifted your fly at the end of the previous series of casts.

Detecting takes in this kind of fishing is relatively easy, because you're usually close to your fly, working with short casts. But setting the hook is not easy. In the first place, the takes are often splashy, and in the second place they happen right in front of you, so they are often startling. That's great, we fish for surprise. But you – or at least I – tend to react to surprise takes with a jerk. That's not so good. It yanks the fly straight away from the fish. Let the fish turn down, instead, before you draw the hook home.

After you've got the cast worked out, which won't take long, setting the hook becomes the most difficult part of fishing the searching dry downstream. It's a problem that is fun to solve.

The Dry Fly from a Moving Boat

The first thing you need, when fishing a dry fly from a moving boat, is somebody else at the oars. It's almost impossible to mind the boat through fast water and mind the drift of a dry fly at the same time. In mathematical terms, they are mutually exclusive events.

A good oarsman does half of your fishing for you. He keeps the boat an easy fly cast away from the best fishing water and cocks the boat at the correct angle so you can make a cast to this water while facing it, not while looking over your shoulder. If there are two of you casting from the bow and stern, and you've got a good guide, he will even keep the boat at the correct angle to keep your lines from tangling in the air behind you, though you'll never notice all the favors he is doing you.

There is a lesson here: when it's your turn at the oars, pay attention to your fisherman, gauge the distance at which he casts comfortably, keep him facing the best water, and call out any holding lies that you notice approaching.

The term *position* applies to fishing from a boat, but it's mostly up to the guy at the oars. You should, however, keep yourself in position to hit the holding water as it comes roaring toward you. If at all possible, stand up. It's easier to do in a drift boat with knee braces, not so easy or even safe to do in a rubber raft. But a rubber raft, properly set up, will give you room to swivel in your seat and face the holding water, which is usually the bank.

Most lies that are best for boat fishing are either indentations in the bank, glides of deep water right along it, or water that is broken by boulders. But many holding lies are out away from the bank, on the other side of the boat, and can be read as obstructions in the current, or else glides of deeper and darker water amid fast water. These glides denote trenches, and give the trout resting places that are also excellent ambush points.

The cast should be made downstream, ahead of the boat, and almost always at an angle to one side or the other. The current along a bank is slower than the current in midstream; the boat therefore drifts downstream on faster water than the fly. If you cast ahead of the boat you slowly catch up with the fly, and can recover slack as it forms in the line. If you cast at an angle behind the boat, whatever slack you have in the line and leader when it lands is pulled out quickly, and you have drag after just a foot or two of drift.

Your attention has to be torn in two directions when you fish a dry fly from a boat, even if you've got somebody else at the oars. First, you've got to watch constantly downstream, reading the water, looking for the next likely lie. Don't depend on the oarsman to do this for you, though a good one will help by pointing out or even shouting about the next place to pop your fly. But you've got to watch what's coming up yourself, so you can calculate the cast. If you don't, a lot of lies somebody else points out to you will be behind the boat before you can cast to them.

The second thing you've got to watch constantly is your fly, already out there on the water. If you raise your eyes to scout out the next lie, that's exactly when a fish is going to pounce on the fly. So you work out a compromise, shifting your gaze rapidly

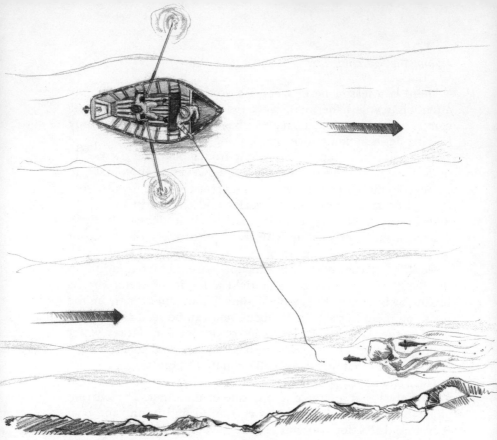

When fishing a dry fly from a moving boat, you get the best drift by casting at an angle ahead of the boat.

from the water to your fly and back. You try to keep them both in focus at once, and you are jealous of trout, with their ability to look at one thing with one eye and another thing with the other eye.

Trout would make excellent boat fishermen.

Mastering the skill of the quick and accurate cast helps you out a lot when you begin fishing from a moving boat. Graceful forecasting and backcasting looks pretty, but a lot of holding lies will scoot by if you wait for everything to become perfect before you deliver the fly to the water. Learn to lift the fly, toss a single backcast, then place the fly on the next piece of water without any extra fuss.

SOME PROBLEMS AND SOLUTIONS

A Fly That Won't Float

A dry fly that sinks is a diminishing problem in this day of high-quality hackles, excellent dubbing materials, and fly float-ants that actually float flies. But flies still absorb water and sink beneath the surface after they've been fished for a while. There are some ways to keep this from happening quite so quickly and to restore flies to primness once they've sunk.

The first thing to do is dress the fly with floatant before you fish it. An undressed fly will float, but not for long. And once it sinks the hackle and tail fibers become waterlogged; it's almost impos-sible to get the fly up and running again. Dress the fly before you fish it and it will float a lot longer and not become waterlogged when it does finally begin to sink.

I prefer paste silicon dressing, the kind that comes in a small squeeze bottle. Dispense a bit on the tip of your finger, rub it between thumb and finger to soften it, then rub it into all the fibers and fur of the fly. After you've mashed the fly up this way, use your handkerchief to remove excess dressing, then reshape the fly with your fingers. Now blow on it. In the old days of wax and white-gas dressings, blowing on the fly served to evaporate the gas and leave the wax. When I first started fishing I used to hyperventilate all the time, and my flies still wouldn't float for more than a few casts.

Blowing on the fly isn't necessary for drying the floatant any-more, but it does separate any fibers that have gotten bound together. It fluffs up the fly, makes it look more like it did when it emerged from the vise, and makes it float a bit better. If you watch an experienced dry-fly fisherman at work, he will occa-sionally bring the fly in, run his fingers over the leader tippet to check for wind knots, then blow on his fly to fluff its feathers, all the while watching the water to see where he wants to cast next.

After you catch a fish, swizzle your fly in the water to wash it off before redressing it. Then squeeze it dry with the handker-chief, rub it in floatant, dry off the excess, and blow on it.

If you fish over a lot of conflicting currents, it can help if you dress all but about a foot of your leader with the same floatant. This causes it to ride *on* the surface film rather than in it or under it. The floating leader skids over all of those conflicts and doesn't drag your fly around after it. This kind of drag can be invisible. If you are having trouble coaxing fish to your fly, or if you are getting lots of boils under it that signify refusals, try dressing the leader. Sometimes the difference will surprise you.

When making each cast, it can help to use an extra false cast, or even two, in order to dry the fly a bit for the next drift. A tight loop helps because it speeds the fly up as it turns the corner and flings water from it. But a good searching dressing will usually float a long time with a single backcast, even if your loops are open and you do not flick the fly.

A Line That Won't Float

When the tip of your fly line sinks it draws the leader and then the fly down behind it. This problem is more common than it should be, since it is so easy to correct. Just clean and dress your line at least once a day, two or three times a day if the water is dirty. Everybody violates this rule because of all the talk about how modern lines float forever. They do float well, and almost forever, but not if you don't keep them clean.

Use any line dressing you choose. The important thing is to remove the dirt, and you can do that with clean water, omitting the dressing. The line will still float. Dressings do make a line shoot cleanly through the guides, though, and improve your casting amazingly.

Refusals

Refusals are a big problem in fishing the searching dry fly. You won't always know you are getting them. One indication is slight boils beneath the fly. You've got to look close. I've seen days when the fly was floating over rumpled water and taking little hops or bounces every few drifts. I didn't know what was causing it until I saw a flash and then a hop and realized a trout had turned under the fly so close to it that the water had raised up. It looked like the fly tried to jump out of harm's way.

Sometimes you have to determine refusals by a simple drought of strikes. Nothing happening might or might not mean trout are looking at your fly and deciding it's not good grub. But it is a sure sign that they are not accepting your fly if they are there. How long do you go before you decide your fly isn't working? I don't know for sure. It depends on your experience on the water, or on the same type of water. It depends on the weather and your assessment of the prospects for activity that day. It depends on your own mood: if you're restless, give up quicker; if you're complacent, stick with it quite a bit longer.

The old rule is twenty minutes, and I can't see anything wrong with that. I know how often I have stuck with the same fly for an hour, out of laziness, or even for a few hours before I finally changed flies and suddenly found myself surrounded by willing fish. Twenty minutes is a good time frame. Adjust it to suit your water and yourself.

Several things can cause refusals. The most common is a fly that is too big. The solution to a fly that is too large is too simple; I'm embarrassed telling you to drop down a size or two, but it will surprise you how often changing fly size, and not fly pattern, will get you into fish.

Another reason for refusals is a fly that is too bright. We select flies that we can see when searching the water, so our flies tend to be showy, like the tan Elk Hair Caddis or the white-winged Royal Wulff. If fish come up to a bright fly but put on the brakes, try switching to a drab pattern. It will be harder to see, and you will have to fish it closer, but catching fish is often worth the trouble it takes to catch them. I had this demonstrated at my cost recently, on my home stream.

I took Rick Hafele there. Rick has fished enough so that you would expect him to know you need to fish a fly you can see well on a tiny stream, where little light filters down through the trees. But Rick started right out with a brown beetle pattern, composed of nothing but deer hair drawn into a hump over the shank of the hook. There was no hope it would work. It looked alive, but you couldn't see it. I thought about telling him he was wasting his time, but decided not to; I'd let him come to it on his own.

I started with the standard Elk Hair Caddis, tan, #14. I got a few takes, not a lot less than what I expected on that water. I was content and covering some water, but Rick kept lagging behind. Finally I waited for him, sent him ahead of me to fish a nice pool, and sat back on a high rock to watch him do it. It didn't take long to discover why he was lagging.

On his first cast I looked for the fly on the water but couldn't see it. I folded my arms and waited for disappointment to set in. Instead, a white welt of water spurted up in the pool about where the fly should have been. Rick set the hook. He played the fish out and cast again.

I didn't see a thing happen that time, but Rick suddenly lifted the rod and a trout started dancing around out there. He landed it and released it.

My policy is to take one or at most two fish per pool and then move on, because the pool is ruined. No more trout are likely to come to the fly. About eight casts later, Rick was still fishing that invisible beetle, still catching trout, and starting to give me advice on how to fish my own home stream.

I got off my rock, stalked past him without throwing rocks into his water, and moved on to the next pool. But before fishing it I nipped off the bright caddis and tied on a dark one of the same size and shape. I took five fish from the pool, proving that Rick's brown beetle was just a fluke. There are no brown beetles on my home stream. I don't allow them.

But the success of those drab dressings was no accident. The trout were bashful about bright flies that day, and we took almost all of our trout on flies that we could see only on occasion after they landed on the water.

There is another reason for refusal of searching drys. If fish feed on a specific insect and refuse anything that doesn't look like it, then it's time to switch to a matching pattern. But that becomes fishing the hatch, not fishing the water, which brings us to the next chapter.

5

The Dry Fly as Imitation

Al Shepp and I floated the Bighorn River in my Mini-Drifter one day last September. Al is a sculptor and instructor at the University of California, Berkley.

The Bighorn is a tailwater, broad and flat in a valley that is broader and flatter. It has quite a few riffles sprinkled down the thirteen miles of its fishable water. For the most part, though, the water is a series of flats from three to six feet deep, flowing evenly over a bottom that is a mass of algae.

When you drift the river and look down into its clear water, the whole bottom appears to be a vast, green, waving weed bed. All of the nutrients of the impoundment upstream constantly enrich the plant life, which is food for a seething of small crustaceans and aquatic insect life. These creatures, in turn, are consumed by the sleek dark forms that quiver and dart away when the boat slides into view over them. Some of those forms are frighteningly large.

Fishing was fair for the dark forms, but Al was doing most of it and catching most of the fish. I was still tired after the long drive over from Oregon and was content to lean on the oars and tend to the lazy course of the boat.

Late in the afternoon we arrived at an island with a channel behind it, and my interest in fishing quickened. I remembered the place from an earlier trip, when trout fed constantly in the channel. It was a couple of hundred yards long, had a riffle feeding into it, and was a double-haul cast across. A narrows and some boulders choked it off in about the middle. The big pool where the channel opened up again below this constriction was always pocked with the rings of rising trout.

When Al and I arrived at the island a big McKenzie boat was already anchored at its lower end. A couple of guys nymphed the run in the main river in front of the island. I beached the boat at the upper end and we traipsed across, hoping nobody would be fishing the channel. But we were disappointed.

Two guys fished the pool below the narrows, casting dry flies over the same rings of rising trout I'd seen on the earlier trip. We watched them fish for awhile. Then Al and I went up to fish the riffle at the head of the channel. Nothing was going on there; we cast idly and let the current push us slowly down toward where the other guys were fishing. Finally it became obvious we weren't going to catch anything, so I reeled up, waded out, and walked the rest of the way downstream to watch the two fellows at their work.

They were good. Their equipment was flawless and their casts were delicate. I watched some of the drifts through binoculars, and even their drifts looked good. Size #16 Pale Morning Duns boated the current; their flies were the same size and were doing the same thing. But the trout weren't interested.

I watched for a long time. I might have whined, I can't recall, but the two fellows quit fishing, still fishless, and went back to their boat. They got out lunch, stood leaning on the gunwales, and ate. I waded right into their water, Al waded in below me, and the two guys took their turn watching us fish while they waited for their friends to finish nymphing the river side of the island.

I immediately tied on a #16 Pale Morning Dun thorax dressing and went to work over the fish. I knew I'd be into them in a few minutes because the same fly had worked on the earlier trip during the same hatch, in the same water. I cast at first with some smugness, knowing the trout were about to get some surprises. After about twenty casts, I drew the fly in, looked it over, and checked my tippet. Both looked fine to me. I cast what must have been a hundred times more. Something didn't look right to the fish.

Binoculars are great for watching ospreys and eagles and stuff in the distance. I also carry them so I can peek into a trout's feeding lane without disturbing it. I focused for a close-up look at the noses poking out of water in front of me. The trout were taking something off the surface, and the obvious candidate was the Pale Morning Dun, still coming down in good numbers. But none were disappearing. Something else was going on.

I watched a while longer before I noticed that scattered mayflies of a smaller sort sailed among the Pale Morning Duns. They made the #16 mayflies look large. Some of these smaller duns twitched themselves into the air, but more of them tipped over the brink into dark openings that closed and left nothing but bubbles and rings on the water. It was a hint that was hard to ignore.

I didn't bother trying to collect a natural for a closer look because I didn't want to disturb the trout. Little Olives are the most common small mayflies on the Bighorn and all the other big western spring creeks and tailwaters, so I assumed that's what these were. There are several species of them, but they all tend toward olive bodies and grayish wings. They range in size from #16, the same as the Pale Morning Duns, down to #24, which is frustratingly small to match.

These Little Olives appeared to be a couple of sizes smaller than the larger hatch surrounding them. I searched my fly boxes for a #20 Compara-dun dressing with an olive body and grayish deer-hair wing. It was easy to find, since I always carry them, knowing I will need them often.

I added 3 feet of limp 6X tippet before I hitched the fly on. Then I dressed it, mashing floatant into all its fibers, after which I used my fingertips to restore it to the same shape it had when it emerged from the vise. A good fly will take a lot of mauling.

I was a good fly, but I didn't own it long.

I cast it up and across stream, at an angle that would show the fly to the fish but leave the leader and line off to the side, to a feeding lane that had not one but about three noses poking out of it. The fly was almost impossible to see, but it was easy to see that the first few casts went unmolested. Things must have looked right on the next cast, though, because one of those noses came out in the right spot, I lifted the rod gently, and the picture of the calm pool suddenly had splashes and dashes painted all over it.

One of the fellows munching lunch on the gunwales of the McKenzie boat yelled, "Hey he's got one on!"

I held on and wore the fish out. It was about 16 inches long. A brown that size on the Bighorn is 3 inches longer than a trout almost anywhere else, so I admired it and patted myself on the back for taking it before I swatted it on the tail and sent it swimming.

I dried the fly on my handkerchief, redressed it with floatant, and restored it to its approximate original shape. Compara-duns are great because they are so durable. They don't look great in the first place, but they look just about as good a dozen fish later – if you can keep them that long.

I watched the water while I tended the fly. The trout were at it again in the same place, so I made the same cast, up and across to them. Again, it took several drifts for everything to get just right out there, then another nose came up, felt the poke of the hook, and turned just right to put its weight against the lifting rod and break off.

Half a dozen fish later I was half a dozen Compara-duns poorer. I felt I was doing well, but was reassured about it by the guys behind me. They kept counting my fish, their voices sounding more amazed all the time until I was amazed at myself. I'm usually the one watching and counting when things like that happen.

I called Al up to help me admire my last fish, a pretty brown with a deep-gold skin and a blimplike shape. It was so fat it draped over my hands when I lifted it dripping out of the water.

"That's over twenty inches," Al told me.

I wasn't sure, but was sure easy to convince. "If it's that long," I said, "it must weigh four pounds, as fat as it is."

"What did it take?" Al asked.

"Number 20 Little Olive," I answered. I got out my fly box and frisked it for another of the flies. "Here, have one." I forced it on him even though it was one of the last I had. I can be awfully generous when somebody has just helped me convince myself I've landed a trout over 20 inches long on a #20 dry fly.

Fishing the imitative dry over selectively rising trout is a challenge that more and more people seek with an intention, rather than happening onto hatches by accident and being baffled by them when they do. It all started in Britain, where the upstream dry-fly cast to a visibly feeding fish became the codified way of fishing chalkstreams. But we had no such rules in America, and our book of flies and tactics is much richer for all that freedom.

NATURALS AND IMITATIONS

Imitative dry flies represent specific hatches. The goal is to convince trout that here comes somebody drifting down the current who looks just like somebody else they've just successfully eaten. But it doesn't always take an imitative dressing to accomplish this deception.

Suggestive drys are often surprisingly effective during hatches if their shape is relatively consistent with the natural, and if their size is the same as the real thing. This is not a recommendation to trot out your fancy patterns when trout begin nipping at particular gnats. But it is an admonition not to stop fishing if you don't have an exact imitation of whatever creature trout are suddenly taking all around you. Try what you have that is the right size and shape and fairly close in color.

Impressionistic patterns, as opposed to more exact imitations, actually account for most trout when they feed with some selectivity. Recall the argument between presentation and imitation, and also recall Datus Proper's resolution of it: *presentation is part of imitation.* If you choose a reasonable representation of an insect and present it so it looks right to the trout, it's usually going to fool them.

Imitative dry flies, exact copies of specific naturals, serve you well when trout feed selectively in smooth currents. The best suggestive, or even impressionistic, dressings might fail entirely in the same situations. It's wise to observe the natural and choose a more exact imitation whenever you have no success with other kinds of flies.

Mayflies

Mayflies have three stages that can be imitated with dry-fly tactics: emergers, duns, and spinners. Emergers are often fished just beneath the surface, but the tactics used to fish them, even when they are fished sunk, are the same as those used to fish them dry.

Emergers are best matched with patterns that are essentially floating nymphs. A lump of dubbing or polypro yarn is tied onto the back of the fly. When this hump is dressed with floatant the fly floats suspended from it in the surface film with its body under water. If the fly is to be fished sunk, the leader should be dressed with floatant down to within six inches or so of the tip, and the lump left undressed. The fly sinks and suspends itself just beneath the surface.

Indications for emergers are not always easy to read. A couple of conditions predict their success, however, and knowledge of these will let you know when you might need to use emerger imitations.

The first condition is a hatch of small mayflies. The surface film is a formidable barrier to tiny insects. Anything smaller than #14 has trouble penetrating the surface film.

The second condition is an unbroken surface film. In a riffle or even slightly tossed run the surface film is rent in thousands of directions at all times. It isn't a barrier. On a placid flat the surface film is not broken and becomes a barrier to small insects. Putting the two conditions together: you are most likely to run into emerger situations over small mayfly hatches on glassy flats. Since flats, with their gentle currents and beds of rooted vegetation, are hot spots for tiny mayflies, emergers are important a lot more often than is commonly recognized.

Imitative dry-fly fishing has traditionally been based on the mayfly dun. It's a handsome insect with upright wings, a slender body, and tipped-up tails. On riffles, runs, and even flats where the fish haven't been pestered a lot, traditional Catskill ties make fine imitations of the dun. Their hackles serve to float the fly and to represent the dimplings of mayfly feet. Hackles also represent wings as well as legs. The tail on a Catskill tie serves to complete the imitation, but also helps to cock the fly at the right angle on the water.

On water where trout are truly selective it's best to go to a more imitative dressing. The Compara-dun style, originated by Al Caucci and Bob Nastasi and recorded in their book *Hatches,* is the best style I've found to date. It's easy to tie and is very durable. It has no hackle, so the silhouette of its body and wing are unobstructed when it floats. The Compara-dun style has produced most fish for me during mayfly hatches on smooth water.

Mayfly dun situations are relatively easy to read because it's easy to see when trout feed on them. Always try to capture a natural and observe it closely. And make sure trout are taking duns, not nymphs or emergers or something else that you haven't even noticed. If more than one species of dun is on the water, as happened to me on the Bighorn, try to figure out which one the trout prefer. Sometimes, fortunately not often, different trout prefer different species, and you've got to switch from pattern to pattern as you move from trout to trout.

The compara-dun style is an excellent imitation of the mayfly dun silhouette and takes trout well in selective situations.

When you've got the hatch figured out, select a specific mayfly dun pattern that is the size and color of the observed natural.

Mayfly spinners are easy to overlook because they float flush in the surface film, are rather transparent, and disappear against the dark background of the water when looked at from above. But trout see them outlined against the sky. Spinners are quite obvious to them.

The simplest, and in my experience most effective, spinner style is the Compara-spinner, again first recorded in Caucci and Nastasi's *Hatches*. The fly consists simply of split hackle-fiber tails, a slender dubbed body, and hackle that is wound around the thorax area of the fly, then clipped top and bottom. The sparse wings represent the veins in the wings of the insect, not the wings themselves. Again, it helps to collect a specimen and match it in size and color.

Caddisflies

The caddis adult is the only stage of the insect that can be fished well with dry-fly tactics. Caddisfly adults have a characteristic tent-wing shape, with bulbous bodies tucked underneath, long antennae sticking out over the bow, and an absence of tails at the stern. Like mayflies, all of the species within the order have that same shape, though they vary vastly in size and color. A couple of pattern styles, based on the water where they'll be fished, do a fine job of imitating them.

The first style is the Elk Hair Caddis. It has hackle palmered the length of the body, and either elk or deer hair as a down-wing laid over the back. That's about all there is to them; they are quick and easy to tie. A few variations in size and color cover the core of the caddis, fish well for trout in brisk water, and even take fish on smooth water except in the most selective situations. You can often clip the hackles off the bottom of the appropriate Elk Hair dressing to make it more imitative.

The second caddis style is the Quill-winged Caddis. It has a dubbed body, a down-wing of turkey, goose, or mallard quill, and a collar of hackle in front of the wing. The hackle is usually trimmed into a V-shape on the bottom, imitating the legs of the insect while at the same time lowering the body of the imitation

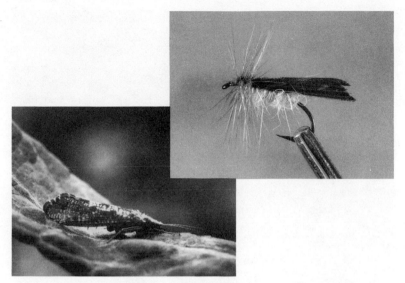

The Quill-winged Caddis is an excellent imitation of the caddisfly shape on the kinds of waters where trout get a chance to take a good look before accepting or rejecting it.

in the water, where trout can get a better look at it. These work best on smoother water.

Indications for fishing caddis imitations are obvious: you'll see lots of naturals boating the currents and bouncing around in the air above the surface. But you've got to be careful to notice exactly what is going on. When caddis adults are visible, or even abundant, trout often feed on caddis pupae on their way to the surface for emergence. They also feed on adult caddis diving into the water to swim down and deposit their eggs. When trout feed on caddis pupae or adults under water, you will swear they are taking them dry. But the truth is they are taking them so vigorously under water that their satisfied swirls erupt to the surface.

Watch carefully when caddis are on the water. If the adults are disappearing into occasional swirls, then choose an appropriate dry, based on the water type and the size and color of the natural, then fish them with tactics that put the fly in front of the fish the way trout are apt to see a natural.

The Stimulator is an effective dry-fly style for the stoneflies. The hackle serves to float the fly, but also suggests constant motion.

Stoneflies

Stoneflies have a shape not greatly unlike that of the caddis adult, though the wings are held flat over the body, and the tails are often longer than the antennae. Dry-fly dressings that imitate caddis often work for stoneflies as well.

As candidates for direct imitation, stoneflies are not standouts. Their nymphs have a great need for highly oxygenated water. The greatest stonefly populations are found in tumbling free-stone streams, where exact imitation is rarely necessary. Stonefly nymphs, with rare exceptions, crawl out of the water before emerging into the adult stage, which is the only stage imitated by the dry fly. It is rare to fish a stonefly *hatch,* but common to fish an egg-laying flight.

Salmon flies, and sometimes the almost equally giant Golden Stones, deposit their eggs, or just hang around in streamside vegetation, in concentrated numbers. Trout gather along the banks and wait for them to fall. They are always worth imitating when you see them at streamside or in the air.

The most effective stonefly patterns imitate the silhouette of the natural indistinctly, focusing instead on floatation and the commotion made by the wings of the stonefly as it tries to escape the water. The Langtry Special is almost an oversized Elk Hair Caddis dressing, with the addition of a thick tail and orange thorax and head. It was originated on the Deschutes River by Judge Virgil Langtry and works well during the salmon fly hatch on any river.

The Stimulator was popularized by Randall Kaufmann, author of several books on fly fishing. It is similar in shape to the Langtry Special, but its yellow body and grizzly hackle are more suited to the color of the Golden Stone, for which it fishes very well.

Midges

The adult stage of the midge is not much of a candidate for dry-fly imitation. Trout do take them, but they take a lot more of them in the transitional stage between pupa and adult, when they fight to break through the surface film. Since midges are typically tiny, and are largely still- and slow-water insects, the surface film is a formidable barrier to them.

There are times when traditional midge dressings, with hackle fiber tails, bodies of fur or working thread, and just a couple of turns of hackle to complete the fly, work well in the presence of midge adults. These flies should be tied on hooks from #16 down to #24, and they should be fished on smooth currents. You couldn't fish them very well on rough water; you would never be able to follow the drift. Again, size is more important than color. You can often take fish just by matching the natural midge with the correct hook size and no concern at all for the color of the fly.

That is perhaps why the Adams Midge is so popular, and the only one that many knowledgeable people bother to tie in the traditional midge style.

Imitating the natural as it struggles to emerge also falls in the province of dry-fly fishing, though the flies used should be fished in the surface film and not floating high upon it. The best dressing I have found is the Griffith's Gnat. It has a peacock herl body overwound with grizzly hackle. That is all there is to it. When

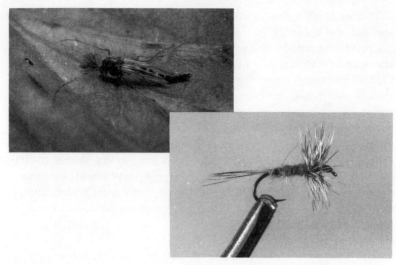

The traditional hackled midge dressing is an excellent imitation for midge adults.

fished it gives the impression of a midge struggling in the surface film.

Indications for midge dry-fly fishing are usually almost invisible. At times you will see naturals on the water, but not without stopping to look for them. That is why binoculars can sometimes reveal so much: a surface that appears slick and without life can suddenly pop up full of tiny creatures when you focus at about ten feet and magnify everything several times.

Whenever fish rise to something tiny, and I can't see what they are taking, I suspect midges and try the Griffith's Gnat.

Terrestrials

Insects that live on land often create excellent dry-fly fishing, especially in the warmest parts of the trout season, when they fall to the water in great numbers. A few of the most important terrestrials include grasshoppers, crickets, beetles, and ants. Others, such as leafhoppers, get on the water and into trouble with trout, but not as often. When they do, however, they can cause selective feeding, and it's wise to be on the watch for them, especially if you spot trout feeding with subtle sipping rises right along the banks.

Ants should be imitated with simple dressings that capture the distinct segmentation of the natural, with a couple of turns of hackle between the segments to keep them floating. But not on top of the surface; ants naturally float flush in the surface film, and you want your imitation to do the same.

Beetle dressings are tied in one of two ways: with deer hair as a shellback, or with a hardened feather tip tied over the body and a slight winding of hackle. The deer-hair dressing shows the silhouette of the natural beetle better, but because of deer hair's sheer density when drawn down as a shellback, it can be difficult to float. The hackled featherwing dressing is lighter, and easier to keep up top. As with ants, you want your beetle dressing to float in the film.

Grasshopper and cricket patterns should capture the blocky outline of the natural, and should offer trout the same impression of bulk that makes them greedy for the real thing. The Letort Hopper and Letort Cricket are excellent imitations.

The Letort Hopper has the right shape to represent natural grasshoppers when they get on the water.

Indications for terrestrial fishing are often hard to detect. The smaller ants and beetles float awash and are difficult to see. If you find yourself frustrated by rising fish it often pays to set the rod aside, get your nose down close to the water, and watch what struggles by. An aquarium net suspended in the current and held there for a few minutes will often reveal creatures you didn't notice even with your nose next to the water.

Grasshoppers and crickets give themselves away when you walk through streamside grasses. You needn't see fish rising to them to suspect that an imitation will draw up some fish. Try casting a hopper or cricket dressing onto the water right at the bank. If a gentle presentation doesn't work try smacking the fly to the water the way a hopper might land at the end of an unsuccessful overseas flight.

TACKLE FOR FISHING THE HATCHES

When we think of matching hatches, we think of flat water, small flies, and fish that are easily frightened. Those are the conditions usually attached to this aspect of the sport, though there are times when a hatch of large insects happens on rough water, and large flies are required to match it.

Matching most hatches requires at least a slight refinement in tackle over that required for fishing the water. The reasons are related to the goal of the game: fishing in such a way that trout are not aware of your presence or that your fly is attached to anything. Flat water and spooky fish require delicate deliveries to accomplish this. Lighter tackle, handled well, produces this delicacy.

Rods for fishing hatches should be long, since length gives you more control over the cast, and more line control once the fly is on the water. An 8-foot rod is adequate and will handle most situations without compromise. An 8½-foot rod is better, especially if it is graphite, since the extra length will not add significant weight in your hand. I use 8-foot rods, but confess that 9 feet is the most popular length for good reasons. The longer rod allows more precise control.

The line must turn over the leader and deliver the fly at the end of it. It also must land lightly on the water. Most hatch matching is accomplished with flies in the size range from #12 to #20. Lines in 4- and 5-weight are normally best for imitative fishing. If the hatch to be matched is a #4 salmon fly, you wouldn't want to fish it with anything lighter than a 6-weight. If you fish consistently with flies #18 and smaller, the 3-weight might be your best choice. But watch out for wind.

For the widest range of conditions, the 4-weight will deliver your flies with delicacy and still get them out there if the wind decides to snort. You might have to shorten your leader to get a better turnover, but recall that when the wind blows that hard the water gets ruffled and trout are not so bashful.

The double-taper line is the standard in selective situations. I use it almost exclusively. But I have also tried the new weight-forward tapers with long bellies and find that they have the fine-tip tapers required for this kind of fishing. The triangle-taper is also nicely shaped and presents a fly delicately to the water. The traditional weight-forward line, with its blunt front taper, is not the best choice, though it will work if you restrain it.

Leaders for matching hatches should be in balance with the rod, line, and fly. I usually tie my own, but recently have not had time, and I've been buying 7½-foot leaders off the shelf. These are blood-knotted to the 2-foot butt section I always keep needle-knotted to the end of my fly line. I buy the leaders in 3X. After adding a foot of 4X as a transitional taper, I am ready to add a tippet of 5X or 6X. If the tippet is 2 to 3 feet long, which is typical, I wind up with a leader around 12 feet long or a little longer, which is about right for most fishing with tiny flies over fussy fish. If the wind blows I shorten the leader. If fish rebuff me and I suspect my leader is the cause, I add a couple of feet of tippet.

Peripheral gear for fishing hatches can be very important. It can also open your eyes to a new world that has always been around you. An aquarium net allows you to pluck duns and other insects from the surface film. Tweezers help you examine them closely. A white jar lid is helpful if you intend to examine stomach samples. A few vials, filled with alcohol, will preserve any specimens that you would like to keep and match later at the tying vise.

You need one other thing for matching hatches: a fishing vest nearly bursting with fly boxes. This is truly not a necessity if you keep the shapes of the insects in mind and select a few pattern styles to match them. A variety of sizes and colors will round out your selection. But I don't know anybody yet who has managed to make it work the way it's supposed to.

Simplicity is the goal of nearly every dry-fly man I've met, but they also know it's nice to have lots of options. The more options you can call on, the more likely you are to have the right solution in a selective situation. That's why we all wind up wearing vests bulging with dry-fly boxes.

INDICATIONS FOR THE IMITATIVE DRY

Rising trout are the best indication for fishing the imitative dry. The rise type is the best indication of the level at which the trout are feeding. If you see trout feeding busily on the bottom, their business revealed by the winks of their silver sides, you can instantly eliminate them as dry-fly candidates. But what about trout taking caddis pupae on their way to the surface?

The pupae dash and the trout dash after them. Often they catch up so near the surface that the rise form extends upward and appears to be on top. Sometimes a trout's momentum even carries it through the surface. There it hangs, almost as if suspended, and it appears to be trying to capture something out of the air.

A look at rise forms can be instructive because it can help you determine where trout feed, which tells you in a roundabout way what they might be taking. With that information you can select a pattern and presentation. Without it you can guess, which is actually a legitimate way to figure out what is going on. It takes longer, though, and is less likely to solve the problem in the end.

Standard Rise

The standard businesslike rise results in a series of rings spreading on the surface and is the most common rise form you will see. It indicates a trout that has tipped up at a relatively steep angle, taken an insect from the surface with a minimum of commotion, and turned back down at once.

The standard rise form and the rings it leaves. When a trout takes a natural from the surface it leaves a few bubbles in the center of the rise.

The standard rise indicates the demise of an insect that has been either riding on top of the surface film, or stuck right in it. Because the trout is forced to take some air in along with its victim, bubbles are left on the surface, at least momentarily, when the rise is complete. These bubbles are an indication of surface feeding; their absence is an indication of subsurface feeding, even if the rise looks the same.

Mayfly duns are the most typical fare for the standard rise. Mayfly spinners and emergers often go down the same way, as do the smaller terrestrials. But many mayfly spinners, mayfly emergers, and terrestrials are helplessly trapped in the surface film and are taken with sipping rises.

Sipping Rise

When an insect is caught in the film and cannot escape it, trout seem to know it. They rise at leisure, break the surface with the slightest disturbance, and sip down the insect. Rings emanate from the center of the rise, but they are few and spread slowly. If the current is anything but smooth, evidence of this kind of rise is difficult to spot and disappears quickly. On smooth water the sipping rise almost always leaves a bubble or two on the surface after the trout has turned downward.

Sipping trout tend to hold on stations high up in the water column. Sometimes they cruise slowly upcurrent in pods, rising

The sipping rise is gentle; the trout tips up, sometimes showing its nose, and the insect goes over the brink.

inches to take as they go, moving 50 to 100 feet along the length of a flat. Then they drop out of sight to reappear a few minutes later back where they started.

Insects likely to disappear in the sipping rise include mayfly emergers and spinners. Terrestrials such as ants, beetles, and leafhoppers are often taken with the same rise form.

Boiling Rise

The boiling rise is a quick response by the trout. It indicates the need to capture an insect before it escapes.

The boiling rise indicates a trout that is in a hurry.

This rise form often indicates feeding on mayfly duns, especially the kind that hop along, fluttering their wings in test patterns every few feet before finally taking off. Trout move on them anxiously. They also take stoneflies quickly, since stones visit the water most often just to dap down a few eggs and then lift right off again. Caddis are the most obvious candidates for boiling rises. They launch almost the instant they emerge through the surface film, and trout have to get them quickly or not at all.

A boiling rise leaves bubbles behind if the take is on the surface. But boils often arise from fish feeding just below the surface. These do not leave bubbles. They are indications of subsurface feeding and excellent hints to fish wet flies or nymphs. They are not indications to fish the dry fly.

A refusal often takes the form of a boiling rise. A trout rushes a fly but changes its mind inches from a take and sends a boil up to the surface. Most of the time it is hard to separate this from an actual take. It seems the fish has struck the fly; you set the hook and it blows over your shoulder. If you get consistent rises but constantly miss on the strike, stop a bit and puzzle the situation out. Chances are good that it's the fish missing the fly, not you missing the fish. Changing the fly will often turn the trick.

Head and Tail Rise

During a heavy hatch, with fish feeding rhythmically, it is common to see noses poking out of the water. The trout tips up to take an insect, then tips back down with its dorsal fin, and sometimes even its tail, coming out of the water. It is not always easy

In the head and tail rise, the trout takes the insect in a graceful curve that exposes the nose, dorsal fin, and tip of the tail, all in perfect succession.

to see this. I recently took a series of photos of rising trout. All I noticed when shooting were boils. But most of the photos, on close examination, reveal dorsal or tail fins sticking out of the water.

When part of a trout penetrates up through the surface, it is almost a sure sign of surface feeding, though at times they feed this way when taking emergers suspended just beneath the film. More often it indicates a trout consuming an insect resting on the surface: mayfly duns or spinners, or midges halfway through the process of emerging. Sometimes it indicates quiescent caddis, but these kinds of caddis are not common. Small terrestrials are often taken with a satisfied head-and-tail rise.

Splashy Rise

The splashing rise is more often a function of water type than it is insect type. When trout feed in a riffle or fast run, they make quick decisions. Their eagerness often causes them to take with a dash, which in turn throws some spray into the air.

This kind of feeding is most common when caddis are present, but it happens to mayflies, stoneflies, and even to midges on occasion. It is a good sign that trout are actively feeding, but not necessarily an indication for exact imitation. On the water types where the splashy rise usually happens, searching dressings are often more effective than imitative patterns that don't float as well.

Ghosting Rise

I've described ghosting rises already: trout chase an insect underwater, catch up with it near the top, and ghost out into the air from momentum. They seem to hang there, parallel to the water, then tip over and nose in like punted footballs.

I've seen this happen most often at evening, in fast water, during caddis hatches. I've never taken a stomach sample on the spot, but speculate the trout are taking rising pupae. Those trout hanging in air make the situation look like an obvious dry-fly show, but it's not. Soft-hackle wet flies usually solve it, fished on the swing. Dry flies are usually ignored, which means the ghosting rise is not an indication for matching the hatch with drys.

TACTICS FOR THE IMITATIVE DRY

When a trout has lots of insects trooping down its feeding lane, it tends to tilt up and down, taking them at comfortable intervals. It is important that your fly arrive over its nose at the time it is ready to tip up for the next take. Otherwise, the fly is ignored not because it's a poor imitation, your presentation is wrong, or your leader is too fat, but because the fly passes over the fish when the fish is not ready to take it.

When you spot a single trout, or pick one out from among a pod of them, take time to work out its rise rhythm before you begin tossing your fly at it. Some hatches are sparse. The trout sporadically takes insects as they come to it, and is ready to rise again soon after the last take. To time your casts to such a fish, just wait a few seconds while its rise rings dissipate, then make your presentation.

When the trout holds up near the surface and feeds with a regular rhythm, you've got to be more precise. Watch it, determine when it is likely to come up again, and present your fly at the right moment. Trout tend to hold near the surface and feed in a steady pattern only when a hatch is heavy. That is when the timing of your cast becomes most critical.

When working over a single trout, make sure to cast over the lie of the trout, not the rings of its rise. It's easy to present your fly downstream from a rising trout. Two factors get cranked into this. First, a trout feeding selectively usually follows an insect and takes it downstream from its lie. Second, rise rings always drift downstream from the take, which is already below the lie because the trout has dropped back downstream to make it. The trout then returns upstream to its lie. If you fish to the rise rings the trout might not even know your fly is around.

Working out the rise rhythm and precise lie of a fish takes time. Hold your cast and watch awhile. There's no other way to do it. But watching trout work is instructive, and it's a good bit of advice to discipline yourself into some heronlike watching even when it's not necessary to detect the pattern of a rising trout.

On some waters trout tick like clocks, tipping up and down to take with absolute regularity. On other waters, usually heavily fished, trout have developed the habit of cruising back and forth in a wide feeding lane, rising at random within it, even during a heavy hatch. I don't know if this is a response to fishing pressure, or protection from overhead predation, but their unsettled rhythms make them almost impossible to pattern.

The best way to fish for these, or any other cruising trout, is to try to fathom the direction of the next rise. Place your fly where the path of its drift might intercept the travels of the trout. It doesn't work often. But it works more often than the alternative, which is to cast randomly.

Casting to a single rising trout might be the ultimate in matching the hatch, but it is not the average. Most of the time our imitative dry flies are cast over a small pod of working fish, with the hope that the fly will pass temptingly over a single fish. If the pod holds fish of mixed size, however, it's best to single out the largest and make your casts to it. That assumes you prefer to catch big fish.

When selecting the best angle to cast to a trout, keep in mind the goal of the approach: first you want to move into position for a presentation over a fish that is unaware of your presence; second, you want to be in position to get a dead-drift float, so the fish is unaware that the fly is attached to a leader. Your enemies, then, are wading waves, flashing rods, or other messages that frighten the fish, and drag on the fly that tells the fish there is something wrong with what it is about to eat. Your position, and then your presentation, should be selected to defeat these enemies.

The Imitative Dry Fished Upstream

The upstream dry is the tactic used most often when fishing to feeding trout. It works best where trout are not skittish and leader shy. Where trout see a parade of flies drifting down to them attached to monofilament, they sometimes turn away from a fly fished upstream because the end of the leader enters their window at the same time the fly enters it.

Fortunately, such bashful fish are rare on most trout streams. Even the average trout in a fly-fishing mecca retains some of its innocence and can be fooled with the upstream dry.

To fish the imitative dry upstream, wade carefully into position at an angle down and across from the fish. By approaching from downstream, your wading waves are swept away from the trout and dissipate without disturbing it. You are also behind the fish, if not in its blind spot then at least far from the area of its focus. If you keep low and tilt your rod to the side while casting, you can approach trout closer than from any other direction.

Your position should be as close as you dare to make it. The closer you get, the more accurate your cast, and the more control you have. It is common to fish within twenty to thirty feet of rising trout when using the upstream tactic. When working this close, many anglers adopt an almost instinctive stoop.

The upstream tactic is marginal but still useful when you have to fish from farther off, forty to even sixty feet. The farther away you fish, the less control you have over the way your leader falls and the way the fly drifts. Long casts work best over currents that flow in an even sheet. If the line falls across conflicting currents, throw slack into the cast, giving the fly a slightly longer free float. But it's easy to get drag out there that you can't see. Fish long only if you can't get into position to fish short.

Once in position for the cast, reaffirm the lie of the trout and carefully size up the exact place you want to place the fly. Remember that the lie of the trout is not where you watch its rise rings drift out of sight, but upstream a bit from the place they first appear.

Before casting, calculate your own exposure to the trout and

When fishing the upstream dry to a feeding fish, be sure to take a position that lets you cast over the fish without startling it with your line.

decide what sort of tilt you need to put into the rod's casting plane. In lots of cases, when using this tactic, you not only need to tilt the plane of the rod off to the side, but also must make your preliminary forecasts and backcasts well away from the trout. You need to work line out and measure the right amount for the cast, but you don't want to do it right over the trout's head.

The object of the delivery stroke is to place the leader and tippet in at an angle, outside the trout's window, while the fly settles gently to the water in a direct line with the trout's lie. The fly should float directly into the window, as if unattached.

Place the fly from one to about five feet upstream from the trout's lie. The higher the trout holds in the water column, the closer your cast should come to landing near its nose. If the fish holds two or three feet deep, and your fly lands only a foot upstream from its lie, it might not notice it, or it might simply let it go by and wait for the next natural to come along for a more leisurely rise. If the fish holds just three or four inches deep, the fly should be placed as close to the trout as possible without spooking it, since the window will be tiny and the trout's focus narrow.

It helps a surprising amount, on almost all upstream casts, to install some slack in the leader and line. It seems that a delivery laying line and leader out straight would be better, or at least just as good. But it's not. Mischievous currents almost always start tugging at the fly right away.

I had the importance of the slack-line cast knocked into my head just this last summer by a pod of educated brown trout. I made alternate casts with a straight line, then a wiggle cast. I couldn't detect any difference in the drift of the fly, but I can count. Five takes came on slack-line casts before a trout rose to take a fly at the end of a straight-line cast.

There isn't much you can do to tend the upstream cast once the fly is on the water. The cast is either right or it is not. That is why position is so important: you deal with most potential problems *before* the cast is made.

Once the fly is on its way down the feeding lane of a trout, follow it closely with your eyes, and also follow the drift with the rod tip. Begin gathering slack line as soon as it forms. Keep gathering it apace of the drift, removing any slack that forms as the fly moves downstream. When you raise the rod to set the hook you don't want to merely remove slack line from the water. But don't draw line in so fast that you straighten the line and take all slack out of the leader. That causes drag.

If the trout does not take, let the fly ride well past its position before lifting the line and fly from the water. If you are casting to a pod of trout, or to an area with rising trout all down its length, then let the fly drift as long as it floats freely, without drag. If you're fishing a glassy flat, let the fly get well below the rising fish before you lift it from the water.

Never rip the fly from the water, no matter how far it drifts out of range of the trout. Raise the rod and pluck the fly off gently, give it a false cast or two, then put it back down above the fish.

When you get a take while fishing over a hatch, raise the rod slowly to draw the hook home. Don't yank it. If you raise the rod gently and there has been some mistake—the fish hasn't taken your fly after all—then you'll tug the fly out of its area, but you're not as likely to spook it as you would by raring back to set the hook. If the fly does seat itself where it belongs, in the corner of a trout's jaw, then a gentle hook set will often allow you to steer the fish away from the pod, so you can come back and catch some more of them.

Be patient if fish refuse you. The drift of a fly doesn't always look just right to a trout even when it looks just right to you. Make at least fifteen to twenty casts before you even consider fiddling with anything.

If the fly continues to be ignored, and you still feel it's the right fly, then adjust your position, or the cast, before beginning that mad search for the right fly. Look for tiny conflicting currents. If you spot any, move into a position that puts them somewhere besides between you and the fish. Or compensate for them by putting more slack into the cast.

Fish refuse upstream drys for lots of reasons. Each of the reasons has its own indications, and recommends you make different changes to solve it.

If you get total refusals, but trout keep rising as if you weren't there, check your tackle, especially your tippet, and check your fly, especially its size. But it is also worth taking some notes on your location. You might be in the wrong position to prevent drag, or the trout might refuse the fly because it arrives at the end of a cast that places too much tippet in the window. Try casting from a different angle.

If you get inspection rises but the fish turn down at the last second, often sending boils up behind them, it can be an indication of some of the same things: the wrong fly, a heavy tippet, or drag. Most often it indicates the wrong fly. The most obvious changes are to smaller or drabber flies, in that order. But check your fly against the natural. Your original assumptions might be wrong, and a different fly *style* might be needed.

If fish stay where they are but cease feeding, it indicates your position or presentation has revealed your presence. You haven't frightened them out of their wits, but they know something is wrong in their world, and they aren't going to expose themselves until they've either forgotten about it or figured it out. Trout don't figure well, and forget quickly. If you are willing to wait five or ten minutes, they will usually begin rising again. It gives you time to figure out what you've done wrong, and to correct it.

If trout not only cease feeding, but do it abruptly and boil away, it's an indication that you've done something very wrong and have to do something very dramatic to correct it. You've got to go find some others.

The Cross-stream Imitative Dry

It is often excellent strategy to cast toward rising trout almost directly across the stream. Several conditions can lead you into such a position, including the simplest: wading depths that deny any other approach. But the cast across-stream is effective in situations where trout have refused the upstream dry. It is wise to move up and try the trout from a different angle if they have refused another approach.

It takes some refinement of the cast to make the cross-stream tactic work. Your cast will lie across all the currents between the rod and the trout. As soon as the line lands, the water tugs a downstream belly into it, and you've got drag almost instantly. A straight basic cast will work at times, but there are ways to improve it.

The approach to your casting position requires slightly more caution than moving into position to fish upstream. You are more closely under the eye of the trout, though it's still a single eye, and you are off to the edge of its area of focus. Your wading waves will dissipate downstream if you move slowly enough. Move into position carefully, keep your profile low, and you can often approach to within twenty to thirty feet of the trout.

The cast from straight across is most useful when fishing close, but it can be effective from fairly long range, forty to sixty feet, if the cast is executed correctly.

The wiggle cast works fairly well when fishing straight across, and it's an improvement on the basic cast, which lays the line and leader straight across the current. Whatever slack you can install will serve as a shock absorber against drag. The wiggle cast almost always allows you a drag-free float of three to five feet, which is usually about all you need to place the fly down the feeding lane of a rising fish.

The line will belly, though, even with lots of slack out toward the end of it. At times the fly begins to drag while it's still above the lie of the trout. That's bad. It is especially damning when you want a long drift through a pod of trout, and drag sets in right in the center of the feeding fish. The wiggle cast is best used when you can single out a fish and make an accurate cast close above its lie.

Mending will sometimes solve the problem of drag on the cross-stream cast. But it's difficult to mend without moving the fly. The most effective mend is tossed upstream almost the instant the line lands on the water. It might seem premature, but it keeps the downstream belly from forming quite so quickly, and gives you a few extra feet of drag-free drift.

It is often desirable to get a longer float when casting across stream. But it's difficult to get a long float because the line lies across the current. Doug Swisher and Carl Richards, in their excellent book *Fly Fishing Strategy*, were first to tell about the reach cast, which solves the problem of a long float when casting across currents.

Executing the reach cast sounds difficult but is actually easy if you have already mastered the basic fly cast. You simply drop the rod toward the water, in the upstream direction, after the power is applied to the delivery stroke. The line follows the rod. The

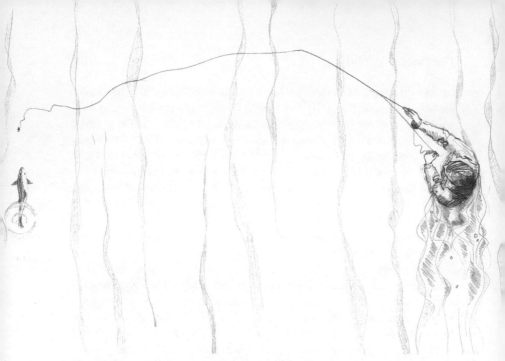

The reach cast allows you to fish the cross-stream dry to a rising trout and get sufficient drift before the fly begins to drag.

result is a cast ˙that places the line on the water at an angle downstream to the trout, rather than straight across to it, installing an extreme upstream belly into the line *before* it lands on the water. Because your rod is an extension of the upstream belly, you can follow the drift of the fly all the way downstream and extend the drift to fifteen or even twenty feet.

But the fly will not be allowed a completely drag-free drift without some slack in the leader to keep the line tip from tugging against it. The reach cast is often most useful when combined with an element of the wiggle cast. It sounds difficult, again, but isn't. All you've got to do is wobble the rod as you drop it over into the reach cast.

Such creative casts often solve problems that can't be solved by any of the basic tactics. Never hesitate to experiment.

A mend is often helpful when using the reach cast. It should be used to keep the back of the line, near the rod, in line with the front of the line, out toward the fly. In certain currents you might need to mend almost constantly, flipping a few feet of line upstream over and over to keep the line drifting as straight as you can.

It is always best, when casting across from the trout, to make any errors short of the fish. Lay the fly on the water to the inside of the lie for the first float or two. When you've got the right length of line measured and feel confident you can put the fly in the trout's feeding lane, just a few feet above it, then take aim and fire.

The Imitative Dry Fished Downstream

Where conditions are right for it, the downstream dry is often the only tactic that will work. It is the only one that makes the fly arrive in the trout's window first, ahead of the line and leader.

The downstream dry works best over fish that are pestered almost to the point of being abused. It is most effective where the surface of the water is glassy, the fish are fussy, and the currents a puzzle of invisible conflicts. It is the tactic of last resort over rising trout that have refused all other approaches and presentations.

When fishing the downstream dry, you should choose an ap-

When trout rise selectively on slick water, the downstream dry is often the only way to fool them because it is the only way to deliver the fly ahead of the line and leader.

proach that puts you in position to cast at an angle down and
across to the trout.

You are now stepping into an area that is just off the line of
sight in which the trout watches for its food. Its focus is still near,
since it is feeding intently, or you wouldn't be stalking it for the
downstream tactic. You are no more than a blur to it, even if you
happen into its window. But you can catch its eye with bright
clothing or any abrupt movement.

Because of your position in the trout's line of focus, you cannot
get quite so close as you can from other directions. If you stay
low enough and keep your rod tilted to the side, you might get
within twenty-five or thirty feet without spooking the trout. But
this cast is more often used between thirty and forty feet. It
requires lots of accuracy and is difficult to administer from much
beyond that, though I have seen trout taken with it at more than
fifty feet.

Your wading waves will move out ahead of you as you move
into position from above. You must take more time. The need for
caution is increased by the fact that you will be moving into this
position only on the most flighty fish. If they weren't wary you
wouldn't need to fish for them in quite this difficult way.

It helps to pattern the rise rhythm of trout carefully when
fishing from above them. This is not so necessary if you cast to a
small pod of fish. But if your goal is a single selective trout, you
need to have its rhythm worked out precisely so you can drop the
fly above it when it is ready to come up for another natural.

Once in position, and with the trout patterned, it is time to
make your cast. It is absolutely necessary to drop the line and
leader on the water with lots of slack, or drag will set in instantly.
You need the slack out toward the end of the cast, not back under
the rod. If line and leader land straight you won't get a good drift
even if you shake coils of line onto the water. The coils will feed
out and let the back end of the line drift freely. But trout aren't
going to bite the back end of your line, and slack under the rod
tip will not lessen the drag of the leader on the fly out where you
want things to happen.

Some form of slack-line cast is needed to put the slack exactly
where you want it, and the wiggle cast usually does it best. A
parachute cast can sometimes be made to make the line behave

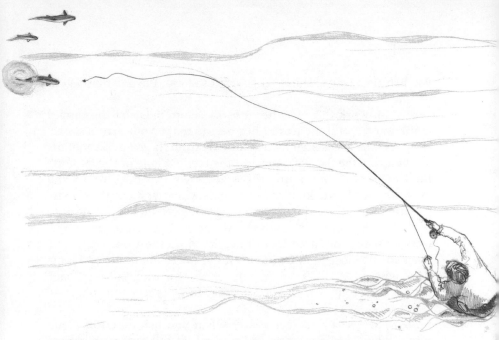

To fish the downstream dry fly to feeding fish, wade into position at an angle off to the side, then place the fly slightly above the nearest trout, with lots of slack in the cast.

right, but the wiggle cast is more accurate and installs the slack with more control. Start the wiggle soon after powering the cast, so that S-curves go all the way out to the end of the cast while the line is still in the air. If you wait to wobble your rod just before the line drops to the water, all of the curves will be in the back end of the line. The result will be a straight leader that causes drag.

Executing the wiggle cast is not difficult. It is simply a basic cast with lots of wobble inserted into the delivery stroke, just after the power is put on, before the line settles to the water. A couple of things make it more difficult than the basic cast. You need extra line for the S-curves, so you must carry more line in the air. That is why a sixty-foot wiggle cast is almost out of range: you'd have to cast eighty feet of line and make it all wiggle.

More to the point in practical fishing situations, the wiggle cast can make it difficult to judge range. You have to calculate the right amount of extra line to carry in the air in order to place the fly right in the feeding lane after the wiggle is put into the cast. If you fish close, say at thirty feet, it isn't so hard. Beyond that it gets tougher.

You can work this out after a few casts to measure the range. Until you've got it measured, it's best to make your errors short. Keep the line and leader away from the trout. If you overshoot on the first cast the fly drifts beyond the feeding lane of the fish but the leader, or even the line if you've blown it badly, floats right over the fish. In the kinds of situations where you use the down-stream dry-fly tactic, such mistakes send skittish fish fleeing.

It's best to tag the fly onto the water fairly close to the rising trout, just two or three feet above it. Time the trout right and place the fly close to it. Don't cast far above it and hope for a long float without drag. It might appear to you that the fly floats freely. The trout, with a closer view, might receive a different impression.

There are occasions, especially when you fish a pod of trout rather than a single trout, when a long drift will serve you better. It's possible, with sufficient slack, to get a ten- or even fifteen-foot downstream drift. But that is stretching things. It's always better, when fishing a pod of trout, to try for an individual fish. By choosing one out at the edges of the flock you can often hook it, play it to the side, then move on to take others.

After the cast is made, and the fly is on the water, you can control the downstream cast to a certain degree. If a belly at the back of the line threatens to extract slack out of the front of the line, an upstream or downstream mend can cure it. If a belly forms out toward the end of the line, however, there's not much you can do; a mend will draw out all of the slack, causing drag.

Another way to extend the free drift is to strip line off the reel and shake it out through the guides. Pile it onto the water under the rod tip. Use the rod to toss it toward the fly in loops or coils. Do anything to get line onto the water and following the fly. As long as there is still slack out at the leader end of things, this method will allow you to extend the drift from your own end of things. But once the slack is out of the leader you'll get drag no matter what you do.

If the fly passes over a working trout without a take, tilt your rod to the side and lead the fly well away from the fish before picking it up for the next cast. If you lift the fly too soon it will burble and reach takeoff speed right on the head of the fish. If you pick the fly up too vigorously the rip of its arising will be reported to the trout's lateral line. If you fish at an angle that is too direct above the trout, then you will not be able to lead the fly off to the side before picking it up.

It sometimes takes a lot of casts before everything becomes just right with the downstream dry, and a trout takes. You've got to be patient and cautious with your presentations and pickups. If you are gentle enough, and your tackle delicate enough, you should be able to make lots of casts over a trout without putting it down.

When a fish finally takes the downstream dry, then you've got to set the hook slowly. A quick strike will draw the fly away from the trout. Wait until the fish turns down with the fly. Missed strikes are common, and speeding up the strike is the most common solution. It is exactly the wrong one.

Refusals to the downstream method stem from several sources, and indicate several possible changes. If you get total refusals, but trout keep on feeding, check for stray currents that might cause unnoticed drag. Check your leader and fly to be sure they are in balance and correct for the situation. If you get inspection rises, then suspect that you haven't quite matched the hatch, or that your leader tippet is a bit too short, too stiff, or too stout.

If fish quit feeding but stick around, chances are your leader has given itself away, or the pickup has put them off. Consider moving to an angle farther downstream, giving you a better chance to lead the fly off to the side before you lift it off the water.

If trout simply flee, they've seen you or your rod, or have seen your line flashing overhead. Perhaps some wading waves swept over them, or you ripped your line off the water too harshly. It's not always something obvious. Often, you've been in their window all the time, out of focus, and something just caused them to extend their focus to full length. You're suddenly in sight and a threat to the trout. Away they go.

And on you go to look for others.

The Induced Take

Most dry-fly tactics are designed to present the fly with a drag-free drift. The reason is simple: that is what works best most of

the time. There are, however, a few cases where a dry fly fished
with some movement works better.

A few species of caddisflies scoot across the water like minia-
ture motorboats. Most of these are flat-water forms, the larvae
living among weed beds, the adults hatching out on the surface
of smooth water. Then they chug about until something prompts
them to take off, or until they reach the shoreline. Trout often
feed selectively on heavy hatches of such caddis. When they do,
the drag-free float often takes the most fish. But there are a few
times when trout seem to insist on some slight movement to
affirm that the fly is alive, which it isn't.

The idea of the induced take is not to mimic all the movements
of the natural, but merely to move the fly enough to make the
fish believe it is living. Natural caddis might scoot in all directions. It is better to give your fly a single hitch just before it
reaches the lie of the trout, then let it continue its drift without
drag. This slight hitch was described as the *sudden inch* by Leonard M. Wright, Jr., in his *Fishing the Dry Fly as a Living Insect.*

The induced take method requires a fly type that can be moved
without popping it underwater. The Elk Hair Caddis works well,
especially if it is tied with high-quality hackle. Wright uses a
Fluttering Caddis with a down-wing of mink-tail guard hairs and
a collar of stiff hackle fibers. His fly stands boldly on the water
and prances across it when drawn by the leader and line.

The induced take is an imitation of life; the fly need not be an
exact imitation of the size, shape, and color of the insect. Exact
imitation is secondary when fishing a moving fly. Suggestive patterns that float the way you want them to are better than imitative patterns that sink the instant they are drawn toward the rod.

To fish the induced take, the approach to rising fish, or to a
working pod of them, should be from upstream, putting you into
position to cast down and across to the trout. Because you will
need all the control you can get once the line is on the water, this
tactic works best when you stay within forty-five feet of your
fish. The closer you are the better you can make it work, but
experienced casters can sometimes induce a take from beyond
fifty feet.

The cast, once you are in position, should be made three to five
feet above the holding lie of the trout. It should quarter down

and across to the fish and should land the fly lightly on the water. The line and leader should be straight, in order to make the fly move. But you must have some slack available to toss into the drift as soon as you have given the fly its sudden inch.

The hitch itself should be small, just a brief hop upstream. Then allow the fly to finish out its drift without any more movement. The right position of the rod at the end of the cast will help you accomplish this. Because the line must be straight when the fly lands on the water, you can't install slack with a wiggle cast. But you can make a reach cast, extending the rod upstream as the line straightens out. Lean with your body and extend your arm, but hold the rod high, and you will be able to hold quite a bit of line off the water.

Lift the rod against the tight line to execute the sudden inch. After executing the inch, drop your rod toward the water. This in itself will send some slack sliding down behind the drift of the fly. When this slack is taken out, you can follow the drift with the rod tip, extending the drag-free drift until the fly has passed over the fish.

Mends made after the movement often help keep the fly free of drag. They should be small mends, flips that turn about five to ten feet of line from a downstream belly into a slight upstream belly. It is better to make several small mends than it is to reach out with the rod and try to force a large mend into the line. One of the easiest ways to extend the drift, after the tight-line cast has

In the "sudden inch," move the fly slightly, then drop the rod and let it fish out the rest of the cast without drag.

fallen and the hitch has been made, is to toss some line off the rod tip and into an upstream belly almost directly behind the fly.

If the fly drifts by the trout unmolested, allow it to float well out of range before you pick it up for the next cast. Draw the fly far off to the side, then lift it gently for the next cast.

Notes on Fishing Emergers

The natural emerger is normally a small mayfly or midge having trouble getting through the surface film. When they have this trouble, trout feed selectively on them, and your fly should be changed to reflect their preference. But your tactics should be about the same as they would be when fishing a dry fly in a similar situation.

Tactics that work for emergers are the same as those that work for drys. Work into position to fish upstream, straight across, or downstream to the feeding trout. The best tactic depends on the lay of the stream and the construction of the currents, just as it does when fishing the dry fly.

When fishing emergers your tackle should be the finest you can handle, and your casts should be as delicate as you can manage. Trout taking emergers know the insects are helplessly trapped in the surface film and cannot escape. They feed with deadly precision, holding high in the water, not bothering to move far from the surface film between takes. When trout hold that high they are wary and spook easily at any movement of rod or angler, or the flash of your line overhead.

Emerger patterns are fished in the surface film or just beneath it. They are difficult to see, and it's hard to tell exactly what is happening out there at the business end of the cast. You want to fish emerger patterns as closely as you can. You will have to mark the drift of the fly by the leader or the line tip. Most takes are detected by watching for a rise in the area where the fly is drifting at the moment.

When you set the hook to a suspected take, do it slowly and gently. Trout take emergers with a great deal of confidence and patience, usually with a head-and-tail rise. Since the fly is likely to be tiny, and the leader tippet fragile, setting the hook hard will break you off if it's a large fish.

Most emerger dressings are tied intentionally for the job. But it's surprising how often you can cobble up something from your fly boxes and make it work. Soft-hackle wet flies, lightly dressed with floatant, make excellent emerger dressings. Dry flies with their wings cut off and hackles trimmed back also make fair emergers. It helps if you can collect a natural and compare it to what you are going to cut up to match it. But failing that, try to get the size right, and the float right, and don't worry too much about the right form or color.

Jim Schollmeyer recently got into a pod of brown trout working over some Pale Morning Dun mayflies on the Bighorn River. The trout refused his drys. He studied the situation and decided the trout were taking emerging mayflies stuck in the film. He searched through several fly boxes, but the nearest thing he found to the mayfly was a LaFontaine Sparkle Caddis Pupa. It was the right size, and approximately the right color. He dressed it to float, fishing it in the film, and took about twenty trout before he wore the pod out.

The Sparkle Pupa didn't look a thing like a Pale Morning Dun, but it did have the right floating characteristics, which means essentially that it sprawled on the water in an appropriately disorganized fashion. The trout took it with the same sipping rises with which they took the naturals all around it.

6

Fishing the Searching
Nymph

Nymphing is more difficult than fishing drys. At first it's not very
productive. At times it's not even enjoyable, especially when you
begin flinging split shot and indicators around and pelting yourself with them. After a few times out, however, when you've
gathered some knowledge about nymphing and gained some
grace casting them, you leap over a threshold and suddenly find
yourself standing in running water and catching trout on the
things.

Trout spend between 80 to 90 percent of their time holding and
feeding on the bottom. When you fish nymphs you take advantage of what most trout spend most of their time doing.

Last fall I flew to the southwest to do research for a magazine
article. I fished with five top western guides in a short succession
of days. Each rigged for nymphing with strike indicator and split
shot as soon as he hit the water. All five constantly watched the
water for indications that some other form of fishing might be
more productive. When signs were right for the dry fly, they
fished dry and caught fish. When a hatch started they matched it.

But most of the time they nymphed, and they took most of their trout on nymphs.

I confess that I normally do things exactly the opposite. I rig first for dry flies or wets, which can be fished unencumbered. My primary indication for nymphing is failure to catch trout some easier way. This presents no problem when fishing is good on drys or wets, because then I am happy. It presents no problem when fishing is terrible with them, because then I switch. It does present a problem when fishing is mediocre: then I stick with the failing flies and catch an occasional trout when I should nip off whatever I am using, add the encumbrances that make nymphing work, and settle down to catch some trout.

Two of those guides tutored me on the Lees Ferry tailwater of the Colorado River, in Arizona, and I learned some things from both of them. Len Holt took me out the first day. Len is retired, dean of fly fishing there, and also creator of the famous Lees Ferry Shrimp.

The tailwater reaches fifteen miles below Glenn Canyon Dam. If you launched at Lees Ferry and turned downstream you would run the Grand Canyon. We turned upstream and ran toward the dam in Len's shallow-draft power boat. The October sun was out but it didn't penetrate to the bottom of the deep canyon; it was cold under the Marble Canyon cliffs. Even I rigged for nymphing right away. It was obvious the dry fly wouldn't move any trout.

Len beached the boat below a broad and beautiful riffle, parked, and hopped out. He fished the riffle first and I stood at his shoulder, watching exactly what he did. What he did was hook six trout on his first six casts. Then he turned the water over to me. I failed to hook a single trout on my first twenty casts, though I did exactly what Len had done. I stood at the edge of the riffle, cast about thirty feet upstream, watched as my bright indicator drifted down toward me, then turned and watched some more as it drifted unmolested down below me. Nothing ever happened to make it hesitate or bob in the water.

"Reel up," Len said finally, "and let me look at your gear." I did. It took him two seconds to figure out what was wrong. "Your shot are too small," he told me. "Your nymph's not getting to the bottom." The riffle was fast, I'll admit, but it was only three or four feet deep. I thought two small shot were plenty, especially since I hate slinging the things around. Len silently held his rig next to mine. His shot were twice as big around.

I borrowed one of Len's shot, pinched it to my leader above my own, then flipped another cast to the head of the riffle. The indicator danced down the current, got to a point straight out from my rod tip, then dove under the water. I jerked the rod up, felt a heavy surging weight, then the leader parted.

"That was a nice fish," Len said. "Now you'll start catching some." He was right, I did start catching some. I didn't do as well as he did the rest of the day, but I did a lot better than I was doing before he told me to add the extra shot that got my nymph down to where the fish were.

The next day Glenn Tinnin took Len and me out. Glenn's boat is perfect for the river because it is light and has such a broad beam that it slides over riffles without getting its bottom wet. About noon Glenn nosed the boat onto a gravel island within sight of the dam. Water coming out of the dam was cold and clear. The bottom was cobble, and I could see it a long way down.

Len Holt, dean of fly fishermen on the Lees Ferry tailwater of the Colorado River, plays a big trout beneath the Marble Canyon cliffs.

The water level had been rising all morning, and the channel behind the island was getting wider and deeper. Glenn spotted some trout working in it and put me onto them. The slot was three feet deep, and the trout were visible only as misshapen dark meanderings of the current. I saw four or five of them that looked to be sixteen to eighteen inches long, and fat. They were nice fish.

I moved into position thirty feet from the fish, straight across the current from them, with Glenn at my shoulder. Before I began casting he checked my gear. He adjusted the indicator, a fan of fluorescent yarn, about six feet up the leader. Then he told me to cast ten feet above the fish and to mend the instant the line landed on the water.

The indicator hesitated on each of the first three casts, but I was late setting the hook each time. Glenn told me to mend my line more often, to keep a direct connection between the rod tip and indicator. I cast a few more times and continued to see intermittent hesitations in the drift of the indicator, but I couldn't get the hook home in time. I got frustrated, and Glenn politely wandered off to do some fishing with Len.

I decided to set the hook as I would with a dry fly: abruptly. The next time the indicator hesitated I jerked the rod up and drew in slack line at the same time. There was an instant of weight against the rod, a head shake, and then a trout hopped out of the water in front of me, long and heavy and hanging in the air as if suspended by a string.

The trout tipped in and took off in a long run, down with the current. I was still attached to it, but it could have kept going forever had it wanted to. It didn't; it stopped when it was a few feet into my backing, then let itself be pulled upstream and off to the side. I worked it into a lagoon of deep but calm water in the downstream lee of the island. It made several runs there, a couple of them long, but I was patient and wore it down. I had to tuck the rod under my arm and cradle the fish in both hands before I could lift it out of the water.

It was a rainbow and weighed more than 7 pounds.

I don't fish nymphs expertly. I'd rather fish drys. But most of the large trout I've taken have been taken on nymphs. After you've caught a few fish on them, fishing nymphs gets to be a pleasure on account of all the trout you catch.

SEARCHING NYMPHS

When trout hold on the bottom in moving water the currents deliver a potpourri of things to them and they rarely feed selectively. Searching nymphs are suggestive patterns, tied to look like the average of what these trout eat. They are not imitations of a specific species of insect or crustacean.

Average aquatic insects and crustaceans fall in the center of the hook size range: #10 through #16. It is not by accident that most successful searching nymphs are tied in the same range. The larger sizes work best when you explore riffles and runs on large freestone streams, the smaller sizes when you explore smaller or quieter water.

The form of the average natural nymph or larva is long and slender, tapered from a narrow abdomen up to a slightly thicker thorax. Many mayfly and stonefly nymphs have tails, but caddis larvae and scuds do not. Some of the most successful searching dressings have tails that can be viewed either as tails or as extensions of the body. The thick tail of the Gold-Ribbed Hare's Ear has this effect, increasing the chance a trout will mistake it for one thing or another. The best searching patterns have tapered shapes that resemble a lot of different things.

Aquatic larvae and nymphs vary in color from almost black to bright green. But most depend on camouflage for survival and tend toward the colors of the backgrounds on which they live. Most common are drab shades of brown, olive, and gray. Your searching nymph selection should cover this same narrow spectrum of colors.

Most popular searching nymphs combine average size, the typical tapered shape, and one of the predominant colors. I use the Gold-Ribbed Hare's Ear to suggest brownish naturals, fishing it most often in a #12 or #14. For situations where the typical nymph is olive, I usually use the Zug Bug with its peacock herl body, in the same sizes. Any of the generic dressings that fall under the name Gray or Muskrat Nymph work well to cover the gray end of the spectrum. My favorite is Polly Rosborough's

Three searching nymphs that cover the spectrum of natural colors include (from left) the Gold Ribbed Hare's Ear, Zug Bug, and Muskrat.

Muskrat in #10 and #12. I have used it for years, have caught lots of trout on it, and fish it with confidence.

Those three searching nymphs cover the basic spectrum for me. I extend the size range down to #16 or even #18 for use on water where smaller nymphs predominate. I use 1XL hooks that are made of extra-heavy wire, both to sink the nymph and to hold heavy fish.

Lots of other searching nymphs are just as effective as my favorites. Anybody who has a favorite and has confidence in it, would be crazy to toss it out and replace it with one of mine.

Many of the most popular trout streams are spring creeks and tailwaters. Their stable flows encourage weeds to take root. The food forms that live in weeds tend to be small and abundant. Little Olive nymphs are dense at times, wriggling in your hand if you pick out a single strand of weed. Scuds are often thick in some spring creeks and tailwaters. They range up to #10, but most are smaller, and can be matched better with nymphs in a range from #14 down to #18. Myriads of cased caddis larvae live in the same kinds of water. Trout take them case and all. They tend toward smaller sizes, too.

Whenever the water you fish harbors small nymphs and larvae to the exclusion of almost all larger food forms, you won't take many trout on nymphs unless they are also small.

I often use the Hare's Ear, Zug Bug, or Muskrat in the smaller sizes. But I also carry Olive Scuds tied on small hooks, and would not want to get caught on a smooth-flowing river without some Pheasant Tail Nymphs in tiny sizes. Small searching nymphs should be tied on 1XL or 2XL hooks, and it's best if the hooks are made of slightly heavy wire, not so much to sink them as to keep them from straightening out on large trout.

Lots of western fishermen roll large and ugly nymphs along the bottom in early spring, when salmon fly nymphs are restless. The same folks use the same flies to pound the banks from a boat long after the last salmon fly has migrated to shore and emerged as an adult. But big trout take oversized nymphs all season long, even when it seems they shouldn't.

Some of these nymphs are almost traumatically large. I fished a few years ago with a Girdle Bug I'd tied myself, casting it over the head of my guide. I wasn't catching many fish. He asked to see the fly. Instead of looking at it he hefted it in his hand to get a feel for its weight. "That's your problem," he told me, and dropped one of his own Girdle Bugs into my hand. It landed with a terrible thump.

I tied his nymph on, but I quit casting over his head for fear of taking it off. My gear was too light to handle the nymph well, but whenever I got it into an indentation in the shoreline a trout hit it.

The heavy nymph did not sink to the bottom, or even near it. But it did plummet a couple of feet before the boat began to tug it. That was enough to put it where a trout would willingly attack it.

Typical nymphs for banging the banks or thudding along the bottom are ugly, and have ugly names: the Girdle Bug, Yuk Bug, and Bitch Creek are among the best. They are tied on #4 and #6 hooks, usually with black chenille bodies and white rubber-band legs. Big trout seem to prefer versions with those horrible white whiskers. I have no idea why; they don't resemble anything in nature. Perhaps all the wobble looks lifelike in the water.

These large nymphs should be heavily weighted. That is the way they fish best for the kind of fishing they are designed to do. They usually carry between twenty to thirty wraps of lead wire, the diameter of the hook shank, wrapped around the fuselage.

Weighting midsize searching nymphs, Zug Bugs and Hare's Ears, is another matter. Some folks say you should never weight them, but add shot to the leader when you want to get them down. They have a point. An unweighted nymph acts more naturally in the current. But a nymph tethered to a split shot will also have some hindrance to its progress. Other folks think you should weight these nymphs heavily and never add lead to the leader above them. The drift might not be as natural, they say, but you won't have anything between you and the nymph to interfere with the report of a take.

I split the difference, weighting midsize nymphs with eight to twelve turns of lead wire that is thinner than the hook shank. The small amount of weight gets the nymph through the surface film and takes it down to the bottom in shallow water. It allows a natural drift. If the water is fast or deep, and I need more weight to get the nymph to the bottom, I pinch split shot on the leader above it. That's the way it was done by every one of those five expert guides.

I weight small nymphs on the same principle, but with fewer wraps of lead: six to ten turns. I believe it is important to get a drag-free drift with a small nymph, and don't want much weight on the hook to hinder it. But I want the nymph to sink through the surface film without getting hung up in it. If I want to get it to the bottom I pinch shot above it.

TACKLE FOR THE SEARCHING NYMPH

You don't need a new outfit to fish the searching nymph. If your light rod happens to be in your hand, that's the one to use. If you happen to be armed with your medium rod, it's going to be perfect for the water you are on. If you own just one rod, it's going to do the job.

The best nymph fisherman I know, Rick Hafele, does most of his nymphing, even on big rivers like the Deschutes and Bighorn, with an 8-foot rod balanced to a #4 line. That's light, but it suits Rick. He does a lot more than just make it work for him: he's formidable with it.

The best rod I've got for nymphing was not designed to fish nymphs. Skip Morris, author of *The Custom Graphite Fly Rod*, built it for me. It's a four-piece graphite, 8-feet 7-inches long. It casts short, long, and at all the stops in between with a weight-forward 6-weight line. It's a travel rod, designed to take along on trips where a lot of different situations might arise.

Its maiden voyage was to the Colorado River. The second day I used it I fished with Len Holt and Glenn Tinnin and took the 7-pound rainbow. That' not a bad way for a fly rod to start its career.

If I were to describe the perfect nymphing rod, it would be 8½ to 9 feet long, balanced to a 5- or 6-weight floating line. It would have a moderate action, neither fast nor slow. This rod would fish all of the small range of nymphs, with or without split shot and indicators. It would handle the midsize nymphs, even when they are heavily weighted or fished with split shot. It would fish the heaviest nymphs, though I'd long for my heavy rod. Most important, it would fish drys or wets or streamers almost as well as it fished nymphs.

The reel is of little consequence in nymphing. It should hold the line plus a hundred yards of backing and have a smooth drag. I don't even ask that the drag be able to stop a fish. I keep it set loose and use my hand on the spool or fingers on the line to adjust the drag. All I want the reel to do is surrender line without stutter when a fish runs. Of course, it takes a quality reel to do that.

A floating line is best for most nymphing. Combined with a leader of modest to long length, a floating line lets you get a nymph down deep enough. It helps you follow the drift of your nymph and also serves as a strike indicator. It offers maximum control, letting you mend or tend the drift. It's a toss-up between the double-taper and weight-forward line. You won't do much nymphing beyond the length of a weight-forward's heavy section, so it won't cost you any control.

A sinking line is handy for some kinds of nymphing. The best bet is a ten-foot wet-tip, in either fast-sinking or extra-fast-sinking line. It's wise to carry one on a spare spool. A thirty-foot wet-head line might be helpful in a few instances, but it is enormously difficult to control on the water. Anything you gain in depth you lose in ability to direct the drift of the nymph or to tell when a trout takes it.

Leaders for most searching nymphing should be about the length of the rod, at most a couple of feet longer. When switching back and forth between dry flies and nymphs, you don't have to make any changes in your leader unless you have been fishing fine and far off. Then it is best to shorten it, and sometimes to make it stouter, again to regain some control.

The exception to the long leader arises when you go to the sinking line. A long leader will buoy the nymph off the bottom. It will also install slack between the line tip and nymph. When switching to a sinking line shorten your leader to between four and six feet.

Rod, reel, line, and leader are almost peripheral gear for nymphing the way it is done today. The essentials are strike indicators and split shot.

Strike indicators can be anything from a bright dry fly to a plastic bobber. Most indicators are made of cork or Styrofoam painted fluorescent orange, with a hole drilled through for the leader. Jam a toothpick end into the hole to stop the indicator from sliding up and down the leader. Indicators vary from half

Various indicators include those made of cork and held on with toothpick ends, stick-on indicators, and a fan of bright yarn. Carry split shot in a couple of sizes to cover different water depths and current speeds.

the size of your little fingernail to about the size of your thumb. They hold up different amounts of lead. Carry at least a couple of sizes so you can change the indicator to suit the water you fish.

Stick-on indicators are also excellent. They are painted fluorescent on one side, have stickum on the other. Wrap one around the leader exactly where you want it and stick it to itself. They don't hold up much weight, but you can see them even if they sink, and they're awfully convenient to carry. They're also easy to affix to the leader when you're in a hurry.

The most obvious indicator I've ever fished was built for me by Glenn Tinnin on the Colorado River. He cut two inches from a skein of fat fluorescent yarn and knotted it around my leader. Then he teased the yarn out until the two ends rose up and joined in a fan an inch high. He greased the fan with floatant. It was bulky to cast, but everything about this kind of nymphing is bulky, so that didn't make any difference. What did make a difference was the way the thing stood up on the water. I could see it from a lot farther than I could cast, and every movement it made was obvious. It was easy to notice a take.

The rule for placement of the indicator is twice the depth of the water. But current speed has almost as much influence as depth. In fast water move the indicator higher on the leader. In slow water it can go closer to the nymph.

Carry split shot in at least a couple of sizes, B and BB. These allow you to vary the weight on the leader to suit the depth and speed of the water. Add weight until you are sure your nymph is reaching the bottom. Sometimes it seems like an awful lot. Sometimes it is an awful lot, up to six shot. But attaining sufficient depth makes the difference between lots of trout and no trout at all.

TACTICS FOR THE SEARCHING NYMPH

The Upstream Nymph with Indicator and Shot

This tactic is central to fishing the searching nymph. It is the way nymphs are fished by those envied fishermen who catch many more trout than most of us do, and catch almost all of them on nymphs. They use weight just above their nymphs, bright indicators on their leaders, and fish with upstream casts.

The water best suited to this kind of nymphing—riffles and runs with moderate to fast flow—holds lots of trout. It is rich for a simple reason: sun strikes through it to the cobbled bottom. Vegetation growth, and lots of spaces to crawl around between stones, makes it a hotbed for aquatic insects. These draw trout.

The setup for upstream nymphing calls for a long rod, floating line, and an 8- to 10-foot leader. If a cork or Styrofoam indicator is used it must be slipped over the leader before the nymph is tied on. Run it up into place and fix it there by pushing the end of a toothpick into the hole, alongside the leader. Most people start with the indicator a couple of feet from the end of the fly line and adjust it up or down as the situation seems to merit.

The shot, or whatever kind of lead you choose, should be pinched on the leader from 8 to 12 inches or so above the nymph.

When fishing the upstream nymph with indicator and shot, mend and tend your line in whatever way necessary to keep it pointed straight toward the indicator.

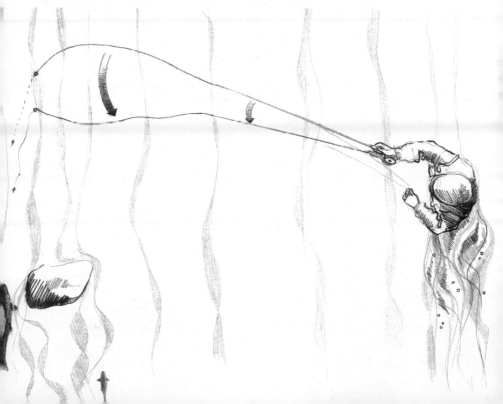

It will slip down the leader with vigorous casting, which gets to
be a problem. It helps to use a tippet only 8 to 12 inches long.
This gives you a knot to slide the shot against. Avoid the tempta-
tion to use a 2-foot tippet and place the shot above the tippet
knot. That puts the weight too far from the nymph.

Your position in the riffle or run should be at the lower end of
the holding water. Wade in about ten to fifteen feet *below* where
you expect the first trout to be holding. Move out from shore only
far enough to clear your backcast and get into position to cover
the nearest water you want to fish. Don't make the mistake of
wading through the seam between the slow edge of the current
and faster water. That seam often holds the most trout. Stand
back and fish it with short casts.

If you fish water that you suspect is largely barren, but has
visible holding lies sprinkled throughout, then fish just the lies
that look promising. Move into position below a lie and slightly
off to the side, so that you can make a short cast to it. Fish the lies
one at a time.

When fishing a broader expanse of holding water, keep your
casts short, twenty to thirty feet. It is better to cover a small
section of water with short casts, then wade upstream into a new
position, than it is to cover lots of water with longer casts. It's
difficult to see your indicator at more than thirty feet. It's more
difficult to mend line and control your drift. And it's almost impossible to get the hook set into a fish on a long cast, even if you
do manage to notice a take. Keep your casts under thirty feet
except in water you can't cover by wading into a new position.

The cast, when fishing with your leader encumbered by indicator and shot, must be almost a lob. A good sense of timing becomes critical; you've got to let the leader straighten both behind
and in front, before you start the next movement in the cast.
Drive the rod through an open arc, so that the shot and nymph go
over your head at rod-tip level, instead of driving themselves into
your vest or the back of your neck. If you make the same brisk
motion you would in casting a dry fly with a tight loop, you'll get
everything tangled. It takes a while to get the hang of the patient
stroke that works best when fishing nymphs with indicator and
shot.

Only in rare cases is it necessary, in this kind of fishing, to
worry about delivering your nymph gently to the water. If deli-

cacy was demanded you wouldn't be using this method. Don't flail the water, but you aren't going to be able to set all that stuff down on it as gently as you would a dry fly.

Line control is at the heart of upstream nymphing with indicator and shot. The instant your cast lands, you should toss an upstream mend into it. This upstream mend gives the nymph a drag-free drift of five to ten feet during which it can plummet to the bottom behind the shot. This is important. If the line lands straight and immediately begins drifting down the current ahead of the nymph, it will hold the nymph up high in the water no matter how much lead you attach.

Line control must be constant throughout the drift of the nymph. As soon as any belly begins to form downstream from the indicator, flip the belly out with a mend. Hold your rod high and lift as much line as you can off the water. This makes line control easier and is the reason a long rod is an advantage in nymphing.

If you get a chance to watch an expert nymph fisherman work you will notice that he is in almost constant motion, drawing in line to take out slack, feeding line out to extend the drift below him, mending line to get rid of a downstream belly. The secret is to let the indicator drift without influence from the line, while being able to set the hood at the slightest hint of a take.

One of the most frequent uses of the mend is to lift the indicator up to the surface. If it sinks, a quick mend will twitch it back up where you can see it.

Each cast should be fished out downstream until the indicator has reached the end of slack line, anywhere from ten to twenty feet below you. You can feed slack line into the drift, extending it thirty feet or more. But that is starting to get out of range, and it's difficult to see what your indicator is doing, or to control the drift of the nymph.

When the indicator reaches the point where you want to end the drift, hold the rod steady and stop the line. The nymph will rise in the current—a high percentage point for strikes. Don't lift the line off the water for the next cast until the nymph has had a chance to swing high up in the water column behind the indicator. If you get a strike at that time, you won't need the indicator to tell you about it. You'll feel the thud.

Fishing out the cast, then, is a matter of constant motion: draw-

When fishing the upstream nymph, keep as much line off the water as you can. It frees your indicator to move in response to the take of a fish and also makes it easier to set the hook.

ing in line and mending as the indicator approaches your position on its downstream drift, lifting the rod and mending as the indicator passes in front of you, dropping the rod slowly and feeding out line, mending if needed all the while, as the indicator moves beyond your position and finishes out the drift below you.

Let the force of the current draw the line downstream and load the rod as if it were a backcast, then make a full sweeping arc of a forecast that lofts the nymph over your head and back to the water, placing it where it will cover a new line of drift parallel to the path of the last drift. You don't have to pelt yourself with fore- and backcasts long before you begin to get the hang of casting without using extra ones.

But it's not impossible, or even very difficult, to make a normal cast so long as you remember to let the line and leader straighten in front and back, and keep your loops high and open.

Each subsequent cast should place the nymph a foot or two farther out into the current from the line of drift of the cast before it. Fish each cast out just like the first: tend the line so the nymph gets a few feet to sink, then continue to tend the line to give the nymph and indicator a drag-free drift. Stay in such close contact with the drift that you don't have to draw line off the water to set the hook. You won't have time for that; once a fish takes the nymph, moves the shot, and sends a message up to the indicator, things are just about over down below.

You must rivet your attention on the indicator to detect the slightest movement that is contrary to the current. This kind of fishing requires more attention than any other, which is one of the reasons it is not my favorite way to fish: I am constantly gazing around at the scenery when I should be watching my indicator.

The movement of the indicator that reports a take is seldom dramatic. Sometimes the indicator dives. More often it makes no new movement at all, but for an instant fails to keep pace with the current. That is why it is so important to watch carefully: you've got to notice anything the indicator does that isn't in keeping with its surroundings. These movements, or lack of movement while the current keeps moving, can be as little as an inch or so, which makes them hard for anybody to detect.

Experienced nymphers seem to have a sixth sense for a take. You and I might not notice all that they notice, at least not at first. I notice more now than I did when I first started nymphing this way. I notice more takes now than I did a year ago. The more you fish nymphs the more you understand what a take looks like. But you can catch lots of fish with the method while your confidence slowly builds.

Setting the hook with an indicator and shot requires a much sharper movement than setting the hook with a dry fly. The fish has already held the nymph a moment before you find out about it. It's about to spit the nymph out. The most successful hook set is a sharp lifting of the rod combined with a quick draw of line by the line hand.

It is amazing, at first, to watch how quickly an experienced nympher reacts to the slightest sign of movement in his indicator. In fact it goes far beyond that. Even I, when nymphing, have at times gotten so on edge and riveted to my indicator that I've set the hook to shouts from my friends, or to the sudden movement of a bird overhead. Once I set the hook to a sonic boom, then looked around to see what the hell was going on. All of my friends were looking around, just as confused as I was.

They had set the hook, too.

When you have covered the water from your first position, then it's time to move either upstream or farther out into the current, and cover another section of holding water. Gary Borger, in his fine book *Nymphing*, called this method *shotgunning*. He recommends breaking the water up into ten-foot grids, each fished from a different position. All of the water within each grid is covered with at least one cast. Then each grid within a riffle or run is covered the same way.

Any features in the holding water should be fished with extra care. I worked a Bighorn River riffle last fall, fishing just above Rick Hafele. He had already taken a couple of trout in front of me, and then dropped downstream. As I moved into his old position it was obvious where the fish had been holding. A slick on the surface of the riffle indicated a trench of deeper water down below. The riffle was only about two feet deep, the trench probably three or four. But that was plenty of difference.

I worked the normal casts to the water inside of the slick. When the indicator began drifting down the slick itself I started paying extra attention. On about the fifth cast the indicator did something – I was not sure what made me strike. But I did and a trout boiled out of there. It was almost as big as the ones Rick had caught.

I'll leave this sort of nymphing with one admonition: check constantly to see that you have enough weight on the leader to get the nymph to the bottom. The most common mistake is not missing strikes: it is failing to get the nymph deep enough to get any strikes to miss.

The Downstream Swing

This is the way nymphs used to be fished when the world was young and simple. Its use is frowned upon now, at times, by those who have learned the newer methods of fishing nymphs, and are therefore entitled to tilt their noses at the old methods. But the downstream nymph will sometimes outfish its replacements on the right kind of water. And it's a lot easier to learn.

The right type of water is a riffle or run with a choppy surface and lots of features on the bottom. It must be shallow enough so its trout are willing to move almost to the top for a take. It is excellent water for the searching dry fly, and most of us try it that way first. But there are times when trout won't rise all the way to the top. The downstream swing with a nymph is a good second choice because it lets you fish just under the surface when trout are bashful about the surface itself.

If the water is deeper than about four feet, consider a different method, one that gets the nymph down to the bottom. Trout are not often willing to come up for a fly through all that water unless there is something going on – a rise of caddis pupae or mayfly nymphs – that causes them to lift their focus upward.

A lot of minor hatches go on all day long, though they never manifest themselves to the angler as anything more than an occasional mayfly lifting off the surface, or sporadic caddis bouncing around in the air. This is true especially in spring and early summer on freestone streams. Lots of different insect species, sharing the wide variety of environments on the bottom of this type of water, respond to the urge toward adulthood but don't come off in the kinds of numbers that constitute a hatch.

When this kind of fitful activity happens, trout see quite a few different insect types drifting along in the current, or swimming toward the surface. A searching nymph fished a foot or two below the surface works well. It doesn't imitate anything in particular, but it looks a little like a lot of things. When fished with the downstream swing it looks alive, and it covers lots of water, so it gets seen by lots of trout.

Nymphs for this kind of fishing are the standard searching midsize types: Gold-Ribbed Hare's Ear, Zug Bug, Muskrat, and similar dressings in sizes #10 through #14. They should be tied on heavy wire hooks, and it helps if they are at least slightly weighted. The goal isn't the bottom when you fish this method, but you do want the nymphs to achieve some depth.

Tackle is simple. Don't change a thing from your dry-fly setup unless you need to strengthen the tippet in order to turn over the heavier nymphs. The rod should be the one you are using, anywhere from 7½ to 9 feet long. A double-taper floating line gives the most control, but a weight-forward won't be a handicap and

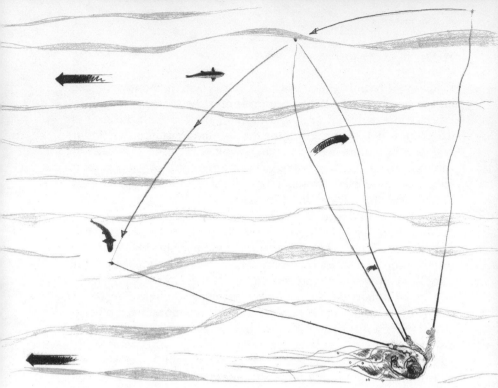

When fishing a nymph on the swing, the cast should be made slightly upstream, then the line mended as necessary throughout the drift of the fly.

might help you cover more water if you are on a broad river. The leader should be the length of the rod or a little longer.

Since you will be wading downstream when you fish this method, your position should be at the head of the holding riffle or run, and not too far out in the water. In a typical situation this usually means wading in at the break where the water first shelves off and becomes deep enough to hold trout.

The cast should be made at an angle upstream, five to fifteen feet above your position rather than straight across the stream. This gives the nymph several feet of dead drift, without any pull from the line while it sinks. If you cast straight across, the current usually forms a belly in the line, and the nymph begins to race instead of sinking as it should.

By the time the nymph drifts down to a position straight across from you, it should be a foot or two deep, and the line will begin to belly. Toss an upstream mend into it, then fish the nymph on its downstream drift and swing. This is the productive part of the cast, where you expect the most takes.

You will get anywhere from ten to twenty feet of downstream drift, with the nymph moving freely, before the line bellies again and begins to draw the nymph toward your side of the stream. A mend or two will delay this moment and increase the length of the dead drift. But trout take the nymph just as often on the swing, so don't be desperate about preventing the line from drawing the nymph into its swing across the current.

You do, however, want to reduce the speed of the nymph throughout its swing. Fast water can push a deep belly into the line and race the nymph straight across stream. Mend and otherwise tend the line to slow it down. The line should lead the nymph across stream, but should never cause it to race. Few insects do that, and trout know it.

When the downstream swing is nearly finished, the nymph will cut slowly into the water straight below you, crossing the edge between fast and slow water. Most people consider the cast at an end then, and pick up to cast again. If there is any depth at all down there in the quiet water, more than a foot, let the nymph continue its swing. Make sure it crosses the edge and enters the slow water. Let it hang a moment. One-quarter to one-half of the strikes I get using this tactic occur after the nymph swims into slow water.

The next cast should be a couple of feet farther out in the current from the first. Fish it down and then across in exactly the same manner. Each subsequent cast swings through an arc of new water a couple of feet beyond and below the last swing. Cover water this way until you are casting as far as you feel you can fish the nymph right. In fast water it is best to use short casts for more control. On broad sheets of water with even currents you can cast sixty feet or more and still fish the water well.

Once you have covered all the water you can from your original position, then begin working downstream. There are two ways to do it. You can reel up, wade downstream to a position at the foot of the water you've just covered, and begin again there. Work your line out with the same short casts at first, covering new water until it is time to reel up again and move to another new position.

The second method is easier, and covers the water at least as thoroughly. Simply work out a comfortable amount of line from your first casting position, then move a step or two after fishing out each cast. It is the same tactic used by Atlantic salmon and summer steelhead fishermen: step and cast, step and cast. The fishing itself begins to have a pleasant rhythm to it, and strikes become delightful interruptions.

The way you detect a take depends on where the nymph is in its drift or swing. When it drifts freely, in the upper part of the cast, keep a close eye on the line tip. If it takes a short jump forward raise the rod and set the hook. A lot of takes at this stage of the cast get reported by a belly slowly forming in the line when it shouldn't, according to the currents. A trout intercepts the nymph and stops its progress. You don't feel anything, but the fish holds the fly, the line draws into a belly, and you eventually feel weight out there if you don't figure out something odd is going on first. Set the hook.

After the nymph starts around its swing on a tight line, detecting strikes is a lot easier. Some will be thuds, which will startle you into striking back. Others will be pecks, sometimes repeated several times before the fish finally takes hold. At times you will just notice a slowly increasing weight at the other end of the line. This is a fish, and it's either there or it's not; there isn't much you can do about it but slowly lift the rod and hope the hook hangs on.

You can fish deeper and faster water with the downstream swing if you use a ten-foot wet-tip line. Shorten your leader to between four and six feet. The cast remains the same, and the way you fish it out doesn't change. Your nymph will fish deeper, and this will increase your odds where the water is more than about four feet deep.

The Brooks Method

The late Charles Brooks wrote about his favorite method in *Nymph Fishing For Larger Trout*. It is an excellent tactic, well suited to the tumbling waters Brooks fished around West Yellowstone, Montana. It is less suited to the milder kinds of waters most of us fish most of the time.

I met Brooks once in a fly shop in Idaho. He was dressed in camouflage, dispensing laughter and wisdom to a surrounding of worshippers, obviously enjoying being the center of attention, just as obviously not swept into affectation by it. Charlie was built solid as a tank, forthright in his writing, confident of his opinions, original in adapting his tackle, flies, and tactics to the water he fished. If you fish his kind of water, his method will work some minor wonders for you.

Waters fished best with the Brooks method are brutal. It works on riffles and runs with steep gradients: rushing water two to four feet deep, with lots of boulders and ledges breaking the current. You almost need to be built like Brooks to stand up in it. He confessed in his writings that many people hated to fish the water he loved to fish.

Lots of steep-gradient rivers flow out of the Rockies, a few others out of the Cascades in the Far West. There aren't many in the Midwest or East. The Madison in Montana is an excellent example, with miles of fishable water adapted exactly to the Brooks method. The Deschutes has many runs and riffles that can be fished with it.

Nymphs for fishing the Brooks Method, such as this Montana Stone, are heavily weighted and tied in the round, so that they show the same thing to trout no matter what angle they are seen from.

The tactic is designed to deliver a nymph right to the bottom and keep it there. The nymphs that work best, notably Brooks's Montana Stone, are weighted with fuse wire until they literally become bombs. They sink like stones. They suggest salmon fly nymphs, and they work best in rivers that have populations of stoneflies, hellgrammites, and other large food forms. The method can be adapted to smaller waters, with standard weighted nymphs, but it will not be as effective as the shot and indicator tactic in that kind of water, with those kinds of nymphs.

Tackle for the Brooks method calls for stout rods: 8- to 9-footers propelling 7- to 9-weight lines. Brooks used lines with ten-foot Hi-Density wet-tips and thirty-foot Hi-Density wet-heads. He cut his leaders short and strong: four to six feet, in the 1X to 3X range. These stern tippets help hold the kind of trout you sometimes hook when fishing the method.

The Brooks method calls for wading into position at the upstream end of the water to be fished, which is fortunate because it allows you to wade downstream. Few fishermen would be able to wade upstream against the current in the kind of water Brooks recommends. The initial position should be about twenty feet upstream and five feet back from the first suspected lie you desire to fish.

With the Brooks method, *one casts upstream but fishes downstream.* The first cast is short, about fifteen feet upstream and five to ten feet out into the current. The first half of the drift, above the angler, gets the nymph to the bottom. The fishing part of the

In the Brooks Method, the cast is made upstream and across. After the nymph has had time to sink, the fly is fished out under the rod and then downstream until it lifts off the bottom.

drift begins almost under the rod tip. As the line and nymph approach your position, lift the rod above them, taking out slack, without pulling the nymph off the bottom, or slowing its plummet toward the bottom. The object is to leave a slight droop in the line between rod tip and the water, but to keep this droop to a minimum.

When the nymph passes in front of you, almost under the rod on the first few casts, the nymph should have reached bottom. At this point the rod is held high and your arm is extended to get some extra elevation. All slack line is held in your line hand. Turn slightly to follow the nymph downstream and begin lowering the rod behind the nymph. Maintain the same slight droop between rod tip and water. As the nymph tumbles downstream feed slack line into its drift.

You can extend the fishing part of the drift by tossing slack into the drift. On short casts a twenty-foot effective drift is all you can expect. On longer casts, as you cover water farther out into the riffle or run, you might increase this to thirty feet or so. But control over the drift is important, and you get the most control on casts under thirty feet.

When the nymph reaches the end of its bounce along the bottom, stop your rod and the line will lift the nymph. This might be the most useful moment in the entire cast: lots of trout hit just as the nymph begins to rise. Let the nymph swing all the way up, and give it a few extra seconds to hang below you. This serves two purposes: it allows fish a chance at the dangling nymph, and it straightens the line for the next cast, which amounts to a lob.

Before the next cast the line and leader should be straight below you, held by the current. Your rod should be parallel to the water, or even lower. After the current loads the rod use a slow arcing power stroke to pluck the line from the water and toss it in an open loop over your head to the water upstream. Violate this and you will bruise yourself. Place the nymph to the water a foot or two farther out into the current from the first drift, so it will fish a line of drift parallel to the first cast. Fish the second drift in the same manner you fished the first.

Each subsequent cast should drop the nymph a little farther out into the current, but at the same time should place it slightly farther upstream. The longer your cast the more time the nymph

When fishing a nymph with the Brooks Method, the cast is made up-stream, but most hits can be expected on the downstream part of the drift.

needs to sink. As you extend your casts farther out into the current from your position, extend them upstream at the same time. This gives you a little longer sinking time, and also a longer fishing drift. But it makes the line and nymph harder to control. You should rarely use the Brooks method with casts longer than forty feet.

Takes will often be heavy thuds, and you will have no trouble detecting them. Just as often you will not feel them at all, but will notice the line beginning to bow strangely, as if the nymph were held while the current continues to push the line downstream. That is exactly what is happening. Because it has happened a second or two before you notice it, you've got to set the hook quickly, or as Brooks puts its, *violently.* If your arm and rod are already extended, which they will be in the normal course of events, throw the rod over in a direction that draws the line against the current, and at the same time jerk in as much line as you can with your line hand. Do whatever you must to get a pull directly against the fish in the least amount of time.

Brooks recommends fishing twenty-five to thirty casts from each position before moving into a new one. The new position might be ten feet downstream, or it might be ten feet farther out into the current, depending on the water and your boldness in wading it. Once you are in the new position, fish it with the same pattern of twenty-five to thirty casts.

Slow-water Nymphing

We think of fast water—riffles and runs—when we think of nymphing, but there are times when it's the best way to fish slow water. By slow water I mean either runs with modest but even current, or long pools that are slightly deeper and slower than runs with the same dimensions, but still have a fair current flowing through them.

In slow water you can fish standard weighted nymphs four or five feet deep without adding any extra weight. In water deeper than that it is best to add split shot and indicator, and fish with the same upstream tactic described earlier, but with a lot more patience than you need when fishing the method in faster water.

Nymphs for fishing slow water without indicator and shot should be standard searching patterns of average size—#10 to #16—and weighted. All of the general patterns work well, but lots of scuds live in this kind of water, and a pattern based on them will sometimes do better. It never hurts to poke around, see what lives where you want to fish, and choose a nymph similar to whatever is predominant at the moment. Trout are not often selective on the bottom in slow water, but they are far more

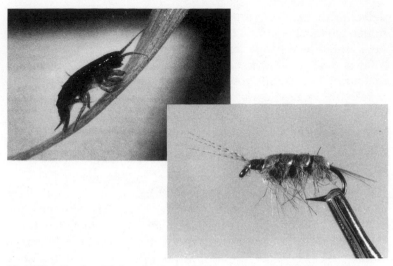

The Olive Scud, with its plastic back representing the shell of the crustacean, fishes well in lots of weedy waters, where scuds can be thick.

willing to take something that looks a bit like what they've been eating than they are to take a nymph that looks like nothing they've ever seen.

The setup for this kind of fishing is easy: use whatever you're carrying. Any rod from 8 to 9 feet long will do fine. Line weight is not critical; it can be your light 4- or 5-weight, your medium 6- or 7-weight, or even your heaviest line.

A floating line works best if the water is less than four feet deep. You can add split shot and an indicator to fish deeper than that, or switch to a wet-tip line. Either will fish the nymphs the way you want them to look to the fish, but you will detect a higher percentage of takes with the shot and indicator setup.

The leader should be long when you fish with a dry line, since the length of the leader will determine the maximum depth at which you can fish the nymph: ten to twelve feet should be about right. The tippet should be long and as fine as you dare: a heavy tippet buoys the fly, holding it back from the depths you want.

The position for fishing a slow run or pool should be straight off to the side of the water where you want to present the nymph.

You can fish either upstream or down, depending on the direction you prefer to wade. It is less disturbing to fish such water by wading upstream, since you usually must wade deep, making wading waves whenever you move. It's best if they are swept below you. But if you are patient and wade slowly, you can wade downstream just as well.

The cast, as always, should be as short as you can make it. In this kind of water short is thirty feet, long is fifty feet or even more. The nymph should be placed well upstream from the point you want it to begin fishing. You've got to give it ten or even twenty feet to sink before it reaches depths where it will interest fish.

On a short cast you can mend line in order to tend the drift of the nymph. On longer casts it is difficult to mend with much effect out toward the end of the line, and it's best to use a reach cast in the first place to place the line on the water with an upstream belly.

The cast should be placed so the nymph gets down near the bottom at about the time it has reached a point straight in front of you. Another mend will help at this point if a downstream belly has formed in the line. But slow water, with an even current, often lets you fish out an entire drift without need for a single mend.

When fishing a nymph in slow water, make your cast far enough upstream to give the nymph lots of time to sink to the level where the fish hold.

The cast is fished out downstream. You should get from ten to twenty feet of drag-free drift near the bottom. The nymph moves slowly, and you've got to fish the cast patiently. Slight currents give the nymph movement and make it look alive. It is best, in this kind of water, to get a long drag-free drift because it increases the amount of time the nymph is in the fishing zone. It takes awhile to get it down there; keep it there as long as you can.

When the nymph reaches the end of its drag-free drift don't lift it for the next cast. Let the current escort it slowly toward the surface and swim it around toward your side of the stream. It takes patience to let the nymph swing through this downstream part of the drift in slow water, but it's a critical time during which you will receive lots of takes.

Once the nymph has reached the surface, or swings around into what you feel is water unlikely to hold a trout, pick it up and cast again. Place the nymph where it will cover a line of drift a couple of feet farther out into the run or pool from the first cast. Repeat the process, giving the nymph time to sink, using line control to give it a drag-free drift, finally letting the current draw the nymph around toward your side of the stream.

When you use a floating line, a strike will be reported as a slight jump of the line tip. It is harder to detect takes with a wet-tip line. Sometimes you will feel them. Other times the line will begin to belly as if the nymph is caught on the bottom. When fishing a wet-tip, emphasize the downstream swing part of the drift, since you can detect takes best when you have a fairly tight line between the rod and the nymph.

The hook set in slow-water nymphing should be quick and firm, but not brutal. If I concentrate too intensely on my line tip, and give a jerk when I see it dart, I often break off. This disturbs me: those are all lunkers out there, every one of them, in this kind of water.

A Stillwater Tactic

Fishing a still pool with a nymph is one of the most effective ways to extract trout from it. There isn't a lot of still water on streams, but it is pretty important water when you find it: it holds some of the largest trout in any stream.

The goal of getting your nymph to the bottom stays the same in still water, but a dead drift doesn't do you much good where there's no current. You've got to impart some movement to your fly.

Nymphs for this kind of fishing should be standards, or your favorites; any that you have confidence in. They should be weighted. You want them to sink fast without the addition of split shot. A weighted nymph will fish at one level once you begin a slow retrieve; a split shot will continue dragging a nymph down until its rests on the bottom, which is all right if the bottom is mud. If the bottom is cobble, the shot or the nymph will hang up on nearly every cast.

If the water is less than four feet deep you can get the depth you need with a floating line and ten- to twelve-foot leader. Make sure that your leader is straight. If it is full of coils and kinks a trout can inhale your nymph, move a couple of feet, and spit it out without ever telling you about it. Beyond four or five feet of depth, it's best to switch to a wet-tip line.

Your position should be anywhere on the bank or in the water that puts you within twenty to sixty feet of the water you want to fish. I have used this method most often on smaller streams, and have rarely had to fish more than forty feet off.

Use a straightforward basic cast, and place the nymph beyond the water you want to fish. As it sinks it will draw down slightly toward the rod, rather than sinking straight, and the extra distance will ensure you retrieve the nymph through water you believe holds trout.

Count seconds as the nymph sinks to the bottom. This is the countdown method Ray Bergman wrote about in *Trout*. His book is old, but not out of date; his countdown method still takes a lot of trout. Count anywhere from ten to forty seconds, until you know the nymph has hit bottom. On subsequent casts shorten the count a few seconds, and your nymph will be where you want it.

The retrieve itself is the old hand-twist. Roll your line hand in figure eights, gathering about four to six inches of line each time.

I won't direct you toward specific speeds of retrieve — Bergman counted the number of figure eights per minute — but will advise you to go about half as fast as you think you should. Then slow down some more.

Vary the speed of the retrieve from cast to cast, and even pause once in awhile during a retrieve. It takes some experimentation to come up with the right magic. When you take one fish, the same depth and retrieve is likely to work on others.

Detecting a take with this method is done half by feel, half by sight. You will feel many pickups, and should set the hook at once, though not hard. You should also watch where the line enters the water. Many takes are reported by a short dart of the line tip, rarely more than an inch or so. Again, set the hook quickly but not hard.

Cover the stillwater pool by casting in a fan-shaped arc, each cast a few feet to the right or left of the one before it, just as you would do it on a pond or lake. Once you have covered all of the water you can reach comfortably from one position, move on to another and repeat the process.

When fishing nymphs in a pool with little or no current, you've got to cover the water with casts in a fan-shaped arc, just as you would a pond.

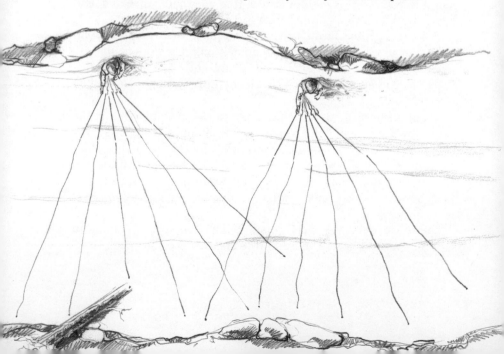

Pounding the Banks from a Boat

Nymphing the banks from a boat is one of the most effective techniques for fishing big water. You need a guide or a friend to row the boat. Craft at the oars is instrumental in fishing nymphs from a boat.

Water that is best for boating is almost always fast. The good water rushes at you, is in range for an instant, then drops back behind you, tempting but already out of range. The oarsman must hold the boat cocked at an angle and about thirty to forty feet out from shore. But he can't be expected to hold it against a strong current, so you've got to read the water right and shoot the fly fast.

The best nymphs are bombs: Bitch Creeks, Yuk Bugs, and others of that ugly ilk. They are tied on #4 and #6 hooks, weighted so heavily they hurt if you drop one into your hand. Tackle should be appropriate to handle them or you're in for a long day. An 8½- or 9-foot rod is just right, and should handle an 8- or 9-weight line. The line should be a floating weight-forward, not for distance but for the extra weight it has up front to help control heavy nymphs. Leaders should be short: 7 to 9 feet. If your leader is much longer, it will wave about too much behind you, making it more likely to whap you on the forecast. Tippets should be heavy, 6- to 10-pound-test. On rivers with willowed banks, guides use 15-pound and heavier tippets so they can yank flies off hang-ups.

The casting stroke must be slow with heavy nymphs. Lift the rod into the backcast with a long sweep, then pause while the line and leader straighten. Use a powerful but slow and long forecast that delivers the nymph at the end of an open loop. One backcast is all you get, or at least one backcast should be all you strive to get. A wasted backcast can mean a boulder or indentation in the shoreline that gets by before you can hit it with the fly.

The cast should be made at an angle slightly behind the boat, not in front of it or straight to the bank. The boat is out in faster water than the current at the bank, where the nymph will land, and where the current is slowed by friction. If you cast at an angle so the nymph lands ahead of the boat, the boat will slowly overtake the nymph, and you will have a slack line during the

When fishing a nymph from a moving boat, you have more line control if you cast at an angle at least slightly behind the boat, rather than ahead of it.

entire drift. You won't have any control, and you'll have trouble detecting takes because of all that slack line between you and the nymph.

If you cast at an angle behind the boat, you have instant control over the drift of your nymph. The natural slack in your cast gives the nymph a few seconds to sink. It will get down a foot or two before the boat, moving faster than the fly, draws the slack out of the line. When the line comes tight to the fly, retrieve it a few feet with short strips. By this time it will be far enough from the bank that it's time to cast again if you haven't already had a hit. Pick up and cast to the next piece of potential holding water.

It is not always easy to detect takes when fishing this way, even when the cast is made at the correct angle off the stern. Some-times you will feel a yank and have no trouble deciding that something is pulling on the end of your line. Other times, though, the line tip will make a tiny dart. You've got to notice it or your guide will scold you.

You've got to keep your eye out ahead of the boat at the same time you watch for a take. Reading approaching lies is half the game in fishing nymphs from a moving boat. Getting the nymph to them, with that one slow and patient backcast, is another half of the game. The final half of the game is tending your cast, letting the nymph sink, and watching for any hint of a take.

That makes three halves. Maybe that's what makes this kind of fishing fun. Or it might be the big trout you can catch doing it.

7

The Nymph as Imitation

Fishing the imitative nymph is a little like fishing the imitative dry: it's not what you will spend most of your time doing, but it's important to know how to do it when you have to. When you encounter trout feeding selectively on something underwater, it's about the only way to catch them.

Noticing trout that feed selectively on nymphs is not easy, which is the prime reason imitative nymphing is not practiced as often as searching nymphing. To find selective fish feeding beneath the surface, it helps to choose water types where they can be seen most easily. That usually means spring creeks and tailwaters, with their clear water and smooth flows.

Freestone streams, including our average home waters, sometimes reveal trout nymphing selectively. The fish are most often exposed by riseforms that are seen on the surface but indicate subsurface takes. But nymphing trout are also revealed by the flash of their flanks as they turn to take nymphs or larvae drifting along the bottom. Such flashes indicate selective feeding only when a specific food form is on the loose and dominates all others to the point that trout become selective to it.

NATURALS AND IMITATIONS

The first and most important thing to realize about imitative nymphing is that one of your searching nymphs will usually be adequate for the job. When trout feed underwater they are more likely to be fooled by an approximate pattern with the right kind of *life* to it than they are by a dressing that is an exact but lifeless rendition of the natural. Suggestive nymphs with working fibers and furs can be more imitative than exact patterns with plastic parts.

It is best to depend on a well-rounded selection of searching nymphs, and to add imitative patterns only as you find situations that demand them. Your searching selection will be augmented over the years by a few dressings for specific waters, at specific times of the year. But most of the time you will fish, even in selective situations, with just a handful of favorite nymphs.

A few nymphs and crustaceans are found in great abundance in certain widespread water types. These are the food forms you are most likely to need to imitate.

Little Olives, the *Baetis* nymphs, have streamlined bodies, tiny platelike gills along the abdominal segments, and long fringed tails. Most are darkish brown with some olive mixed in. They range in size from #14 down to #20, but #16 is most common. They are found in almost all moving water types: riffles, runs, pools, and up under the banks. But they are most abundant in water with gentle currents and rooted vegetation: spring creeks and tailwaters.

It seems ironic that our richest waters have the largest populations of the smallest insects, and are best fished with small nymphs. The standard Pheasant Tail, mentioned earlier as a searching pattern, is the best imitative pattern in waters where Little Olive nymphs are thick. That is the reason the Pheasant Tail is an excellent searching pattern: it is a good imitation of prolific *Baetis* naturals.

Caddisfly larvae of the predaceous type are never quite so abundant as Little Olive nymphs, but they do dominate lots of riffles, and can be just as important to the fisherman. They are commonly called green rock worms, and their name gives away both their color and their shape. They vary in shades from pale

The Pheasant Tail nymph is an excellent searching pattern, but also serves as a specific imitation of *Baetis* mayfly nymphs, which are abundant in tailwaters and spring creeks.

olive to an almost neon green. Their shape is wormlike, though they have short legs and distinct heads.

Green rock worms don't often show themselves to the casual observer. You've got to get into a riffle and turn over stones before you begin to notice them. But trout notice them all the time. Because they are restless hunters, and can't swim, these larvae often get dislodged into the currents where they tumble helplessly along the bottom.

The best imitation, the Green Caddis Larva, is tied on hooks with curved shanks. Sizes #10 through #14 are generally best, and should be weighted heavily to get them to the bottom.

Caddis pupae can be important in all kinds of water. They are such a brief transitional stage that it's hard to tell when trout feed on them. But I've seen times when a trout, caught and held in the hand to be unhooked, has gorged until caddis pupae literally crawl around in its mouth.

Caddis pupae arise from all types of water. They are abundant in riffles and runs. But many types thrive in weed beds, adapting to slower currents and more stable seasonal flows. Trout often concentrate on the pupae during an emergence, completely ignoring hatched caddis adults.

Imitations for caddis pupae should be based on Gary LaFontaine's research, revealed in his book *Caddisflies*. His Sparkle Pupa patterns capture bubbles of air and reflect points of light. LaFontaine writes that four primary color schemes cover 70 percent of caddis hatches, which agrees with my philosophy that a specific nymph style, tied in a narrow range of colors and sizes, will often serve you better than a confusion of them. LaFontaine's four basic colors are the Brown and Yellow Pupa, Brown and Bright Green Pupa, Dark Gray Pupa, and Ginger Pupa. They are tied on standard shank hooks, weighted to get them down.

Stonefly nymphs are in actuality so seldom concentrated that they rarely cause selective feeding. That will be viewed as a heretical statement by some fishermen, but I think most will agree that the majority of stonefly species get through life being sniped at constantly by trout, but are rarely fed on selectively.

The exception is the giant salmon fly nymph during its spring migration toward shore for emergence. Salmon flies are not adapted to many waters, but the few that are perfect for them — the Deschutes, Madison, Big Hole, and Yellowstone, among others — have such great populations that trout get snooty about

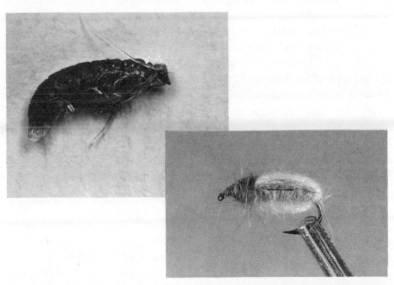

The LaFontaine Sparkle Pupa is the best imitation style for caddis pupae when trout feed on them selectively.

flies that don't resemble them. The key, however, is *resemblance.*
You don't need an exact imitation.

Any fly from a Black Woolly Worm to a Bitch Creek Nymph
will turn a trout's head when salmon fly nymphs are on the
march across the bottom. Other favorites include the Montana
Stone and Box Canyon Stone.

Midge larvae are often taken by trout, but not often selectively.
Midge pupae, on the other hand, concentrate during an emergence and are defenseless against trout. They rise feebly toward
the top. They are so small that the surface film is a major barrier
to them, causing them to hang helplessly while trout cruise
along, picking them like tiny berries.

Their numbers are greatest, and they are most vulnerable to
trout, where the water is gentlest. That takes us back to the same
water type where we've already found the most important
mayfly and caddisfly hatches: spring creeks and stable tailwaters. You begin to see that most situations requiring imitative
nymphing happen on that kind of water.

Imitations of midge pupae don't need to be very detailed, but
they do need to have the right size and shape. Traditional Midge
Pupae do a fine job of imitating them. Most are tied on #16 to #20
hooks, and a narrow range of colors will cover most hatches. I
have encountered them most often in shades of olive, tan, and
black.

Scuds are prolific in favorable water, and it helps to match
them where their populations are greatest. They can be found in
some numbers in most waters, but they are most abundant in
slow, weedy waters.

Dressings that fish well for scuds usually incorporate some sort
of shellback to capture the look of the crustacean's skin. The
naturals also have a myriad of tiny swimming paddles, lined up
in twin rows along their undersides. When a scud swims, these
paddles whirr, but they are so small that it looks as if the scud is
driven by an invisible propeller. Scuds are always curved when
you capture them, but always straight when paddling through
the water. They look like animated little sticks.

That's the way trout see them, and the flies that match them
best are tied on hooks with straight shanks, in sizes #10 through
#14. I have found the Olive Scud and Len Holt's Lees Ferry
Shrimp most important in my own fishing.

That is a narrow range of naturals, and a small number of flies to match them. You might encounter others important on your home waters, or on other waters. Observation and flexibility in imitation are important whenever you begin to solve selective situations.

TACTICS FOR IMITATIVE NYMPHS

Many tactics used to fish imitative nymphs are based on similar tactics used to fish dry flies or searching nymphs. There are always differences when fishing to trout feeding selectively beneath the surface, but most of the methods covered in this chapter are related to those covered in earlier chapters.

Upstream Nymphing to Subsurface Feeders

When trout hold high in the water column and feed visibly just beneath the surface, they often take insects rising toward the surface for emergence. This happens most often with mayflies and midges, less frequently with caddisflies, rarely with stoneflies. One of the clues to what is going on is the sporadic presence of some kind of adult insect. Usually you will see a few mayfly duns boating the currents, a few midge adults lifting into the air, or a few caddis adults bouncing above the water, all of them ignored by the trout.

Subsurface feeding often happens during the early stages of a hatch, when lots of nymphs or pupae begin rising but not all of them make it to the top. More start than finish, and the difference is made up by feeding trout. Fish follow such activity, starting on the bottom and sliding higher in the water as the concentration of insects moves up in the water column. When the highest concentration of insects finally reaches the surface, trout normally turn their attention to the top, and it's best to fish dry flies.

A period of subsurface feeding does not happen during every hatch. The period can be brief and transitional, or just not noticed until it's about over. At other times it goes on for hours. If you don't recognize it and solve it you can fish in frustration until you give up and quit.

The best way to recognize subsurface nymphing is to quit casting and watch the trout. Are the rises into which you've been pasting your dry flies actually boils surging up to the surface? Are there a few true surface feeders while most of the fish betray themselves with winks as they feed underwater? Are the few adult insects on the water drifting along unmolested?

Nymphs for these situations should suggest the naturals trout are taking. Sometimes you will have to approach imitation with fair exactness to take many trout, but such times are not as common as you might think. Often you already own a nymph that will solve the situation, if it is fished right.

Flies for fishing barely subsurface should be lightly weighted, just enough to break them through the surface film and get them down a few inches. Six to ten turns of lead wire the diameter of the hook shank accomplish this. Most experienced nymph fishermen who tie their own flies weight them lightly and depend on the addition of split shot to get the nymph deeper when they want to fish it on the bottom.

The upstream tactic with a shallow nymph can be used on riffles, but will be called into play more often on smooth runs and flats. Tackle should be exactly what you would use for dry-fly fishing in the same water. All you've got to do is nip off the floating fly and tie on the nymph. It often helps to rub two-thirds of the leader with floatant to hold the fly higher in the water and to help you detect takes.

Your casting position should be below the feeding fish and off to the side. Move in as close as you can; you will not have the advantage of watching a fish come up for your dry fly. The signs of a take will be subtle, and you will need to be closer, and more attentive, to notice them.

The presentation should be as delicate as it would be with a dry fly. The nymph should enter the water two to ten feet above the feeding fish. If you work a pod of trout, then the fly should fall to the water upstream from the fish that is farthest, so that it can fish downstream through the others. It is usually best, even over a pod of fish, to work on one at a time. You are less likely to frighten a single fish and send the flock flying.

It is preferable, as in dry-fly fishing, to place the cast on the water from an angle off to the side of the fish, so that the line and leader tip remain out of the trout's window. If you make an error be sure the cast is short, not long, so the fish is not lined. Work

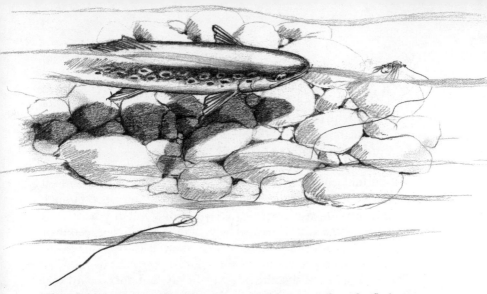

When fishing the imitative nymph to a visible trout, place the fly just as carefully on the water as you would a dry, and be sure the line and leader drift off to the side of the fish, not over the top of it.

out your distances carefully, making two or three short casts if necessary. The trout might surprise you and turn to take one of these preliminary casts.

If you can't get into a position that eliminates drag, then use a slack-line cast, just as you would with a dry fly. You might find it useful to make a mend after the line is on the water, but mending is usually more useful on a cast across current than it is when casting at an angle upstream.

Fish out the cast exactly as you would with a dry fly. Gather slack as it develops in the line on the water. Keep your rod low so that you can raise it to set the hook. Don't lift the nymph from the water, if the fish fails to take it, until it has drifted well below the lie. Be gentle when you do lift it for the next cast; you don't want to send any alarming messages to the trout's lateral line.

Repeat your cast several times, at least fifteen or twenty. With a dry fly it is easier to see if you've gotten a good drift. When fishing a nymph it is difficult to tell if the fly drifts just the way you want it to, so it's best to give it lots of chances. Rarely will you know why the tenth cast looked different than the first cast, but the trout might turn to take the fly as if all those other casts hadn't happened.

The signs of a take can be obvious. Often it's a rise just as if the trout took a dry. If you spot a rise near your fly, raise the rod to set the hook. Sometimes it will be a false alarm, but you need to know, and there's only one way to find out. The closer you can mind the drift of your fly the better you will be able to separate strikes from fish taking naturals near your fly.

Signs of a subsurface take are often subtle. Sometimes all you see is an underwater wink, or some sixth sense tells you to lift the rod. At other times, especially if the trout are deep enough that their movements are obscure, you must watch where your leader enters the water, or watch your line tip. If the leader or line makes an unusual movement, hesitating in the current or darting upstream against it, set the hook.

The hook set should come quickly, firmly, but not so hard that a miss rips the line off the water. It is easy to put fish down when they feed just subsurface. All of your movements, from casting the fly to setting the hook, should be slow to avoid frightening the fish.

The Cross-stream Imitative Nymph

If this tactic sounds a lot like the cross-stream dry fly, that's because it is. The method is almost identical; the flies fished are different.

The fish, in this case, feed a few inches beneath the surface. At times they are deeper, but the method is not as effective if they are more than a couple of feet down. On some water so clear that you can watch the fish, the cross-stream method will work on fish feeding three or four feet down. But it's usually more effective to fish such situations with an indicator and shot, and an upstream cast.

Nymphs used in this kind of fishing should be weighted. As in the upstream method, a few turns of lead wire help the fly penetrate the surface film. You don't want it plunging down, but you do want it to sink slowly and reach the level of feeding trout.

Naturals with behavior indicating this method include mayfly nymphs, midge pupae, and caddis pupae. Nymphs that are most effective are the Pheasant Tail, traditional midge pupal patterns, and the series of LaFontaine Sparkle Caddis Pupae. Collecting a specimen and matching it with a suggestion of its size, form, and color will always increase your chances when fish feed selectively.

This method works best in smooth and clear currents where fish are visible when they feed high in the water column. The tactic itself would be just as effective in riffled water, but trout rarely hold high in fast water.

Your tackle setup should be the same you would use when dry-fly fishing in the same conditions. Again, no changes need be made, though it can help to dress the upper two-thirds of the leader. It can also help to add an indicator if the trout hold more than a foot or so deep.

Your position should be directly across from the feeding fish. The closer you get, the more accurate your presentation will be, and the better you will be able to follow the drift of your fly.

The cast itself should be delicate, and should place the fly a few feet upstream from the trout, in line with its lie. If the fish holds near the surface, the nymph should be placed just above its lie. If the fish holds deeper, cast farther upstream, calculating the dis-

To fish a nymph across stream to visible or feeding trout, use the reach cast just as you would with a dry fly, to get a longer drag-free drift.

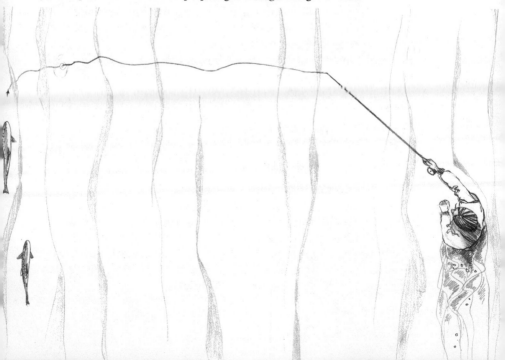

tance needed to let the fly sink to the level of the fish. Again, if you make errors, try to make them short of the fish, rather than overcasting and lining it. The short cast will seldom frighten a trout and might cause it to turn for a take. The long cast, across the trout's bow, can put it down.

A reach cast will often serve you well when fishing across stream to nymphing trout, just as it does when fishing drys. Make the normal forward cast, but tip your rod over and reach upstream while the line straightens out in the air. The line will fall at an angle downstream toward the fish. Follow the drift downstream with your rod, and you can extend your drift several feet.

A slack-line cast is also worth considering. If the line and leader land straight, with no slack to feed into the drift of the nymph, the fly will act unnaturally. This does not cause the problems it does with dry flies; trout are used to seeing submerged insects being tugged by currents. But too large a movement in conflict with the current will alarm trout and make them refuse the nymph.

When fishing across stream, line control becomes very important. Use mends to tend the line over conflicting currents, or feed out line to extend the drift. Line control with a nymph should be much the same as line control when fishing a dry fly: keep the nymph moving freely as long as you can, especially in the area where it approaches feeding trout.

Fish out the cast until it is well beyond the trout. If the fish is one of a pod, or is in water that looks like it might hold other trout that you can't see, then fish out the cast as long as the fly acts like a natural. Don't pick it up until it has outlived its prospects of attracting a trout.

Repeat the cast several times to the same fish. Fiddle slightly with the length of the cast, and with the distance you drop the fly above the fish. It often takes some juggling to get everything just right, in the eyes of the trout.

The take to a cross-stream nymph will be delicate. You are unlikely to feel it. You will often see the trout turn, or notice the flash of white as it opens and closes its mouth. Most of the time you will notice no more than a slight hesitation where the leader enters the water, or a tiny jump forward at the line tip. When something tips you off, set the hook quickly.

The Rosborough Method

In his *Tying and Fishing the Fuzzy Nymphs*, Polly Rosborough outlines a method that I've not read about anywhere else. It could be called *fishing under the hatch*, but I think it needs the famous man's name attached to it, so I've called it the Rosborough method here.

It puzzled Polly that lots of trout rose during a hatch, and were easy enough to take with dry flies, but the bigger trout that he knew held in his favorite rivers didn't come to the same drys. He suspected that big trout must take advantage of all that insect activity. But they didn't show up in the catch. Where were they?

After quite a bit of working the problem to a conclusion, he discovered that the bigger trout were right where they belonged, almost in the thick of things. But their natural caution, which had enabled them to stick around long enough to grow large, kept them down in the water column, continuing to feed on nymphs under the hatch while smaller trout moved up to feed on

The Rosborough Method is designed to catch large trout that continue feeding on nymphs under a hatch while small fish feed on the surface.

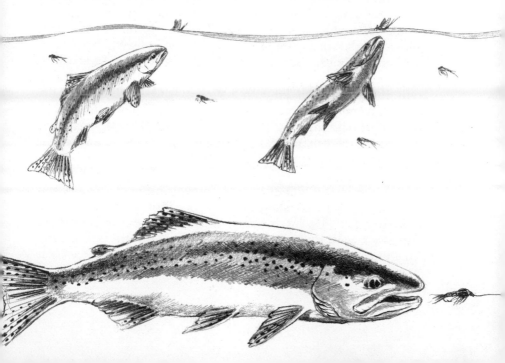

drys. Polly worked out a method for taking those bigger trout. He created flies and tactics to imitate nymphs as they rose toward the surface to emerge.

Polly's waters are mostly gentle, low-gradient streams on the east slopes of Oregon's southern Cascade Mountains. They have wide sweeps of current with steady, even flow. They also have heavy populations of large mayflies and stoneflies. His dressings are slender, dressed on long-shank hooks, and unweighted. The Near Enough and Black Drake are favorite examples, tied on size #10 and #12 hooks, with natural furs that are teased out to make them fuzzy. Polly is obviously a proponent of *fuzzy*, lifelike flies: you can tell by the title of his book.

The tackle setup for Polly's method is about the same as that for dry-fly fishing, except that the leader is somewhat stouter. It should be in balance with the fairly large nymphs being cast and about the length of the rod. A dry line suits the method best, though a wet-tip line gets the fly deeper without sacrificing too much control.

The casting position is taken across stream and slightly above trout feeding on the surface. Remember that the nymph should fish under these, with the hope that a larger trout is down there somewhere feeding on natural nymphs. The cast is made up and across the stream, from ten to twenty feet above the suspected lie of the trout you want to catch. This first portion of the drift allows the nymph to sink, before you begin to fish it.

After the fly has had its ten to twenty feet of drag-free drift in order to get it down, it should be fished out with a cross-stream swing. The rod is teased with a slow pulsing rhythm while the nymph completes its swing. I have watched Polly fish his flies this way; he is intent on what is going on out there. He seems to be coaxing the fish, his rod working up and down in a way that makes you imagine the fly darting ahead, then resting, then darting ahead again.

This is a perfect imitation of the movement made by a swimmer mayfly nymph: a short burst of speed, then rest, then burst forward again. During a hatch, their movement is across the current, toward shallow water, and upward toward the surface. That's exactly the direction taken by the fly as Polly teases it through its swing.

A take in this kind of fishing is not difficult to detect. The fish is convinced; it takes with a thump. And as Polly predicts, it is normally larger than the trout taking duns off the surface.

The Induced Take

The induced take tactic with a nymph is similar to the induced take method in dry-fly fishing. It is used for similar reasons, and with the hope of similar results: a trout drawn to the fly because of its lifelike movement. The tactic was worked out by the late Frank Sawyer, long a riverkeeper on the Avon in England.

Sawyer noticed that trout feeding in a drift line saw lots of tiny particles drifting past them. Some of it revealed life and was taken. Some did not, and was not. He reasoned that a small movement made by the nymph at the right moment would separate it from objects that drifted inertly. It would give the impression of life and induce a take. It worked.

Water suited to the method is limited. It has got to be so smooth and clear that you can spot your fish, stalk it, and observe it while it feeds. That limits the method to spring creeks, some tailwaters, and a few freestone situations where trout feed visibly in low, clear water. Such situations are not common in most trout fishing. But when one is encountered the induced-take method often solves it.

Nymphs used to prompt an induced take are small. The traditional dressing associated with Sawyer and his method is the Pheasant Tail, which he ties with copper wire instead of tying thread. The wire gives the fly an added bit of sturdiness and boosts its sink rate. The imitation is based on nymphs of the British Olives, which are related to our own Little Olives. But the Pheasant Tail, as Sawyer pointed out in *The Masters on the Nymph,* can represent a lot of different things to a feeding trout.

The tackle setup should be delicate, and the same as that used for dry-fly fishing in the same kind of water. The rod should be 8½ to 9 feet long, the line a floating double-taper from 4- to 6-weight. The leader should be long and fine, its upper two-thirds dressed with floatant.

The position for the cast is below the feeding fish. The cast is made up and across stream. The fly is placed on the water a

The slight movement of a nymph, in the induced take technique, separates it as something living from the dead things around it.

couple of feet above the feeding fish, in line with it, or just short of the drift line leading to it. Errors should be made short to avoid showing the leader and line to the fish. The nymph is allowed to drift and sink briefly, before any movement is made. Gather any slack off the water, and hold the rod low.

The movement for the induced take, according to Sawyer, should be made close enough to the fish "to come as a kind of surprise." When the fly is within a foot of the position of the fish, raise the rod slowly, with an even but not abrupt lift of about a foot. This gives the fly a slight movement in the water, right under the trout's eye.

The take will rarely be felt, but you can often see the trout turn, or even notice the white flash as it opens and closes its jaws to inhale the fly. Raise the rod quickly if you notice any hint of a take.

Sawyer recommends watching intently where the leader enters the water. If there is any hesitation, or if the leader suddenly jumps or sinks, set the hook with a quick upward flick. The fish will reject the nymph as soon as it detects the unusual texture, which will be a matter of seconds. This means that things are happening fast out there and they need to happen even faster at your end if you are going to get the hook into the trout.

8

Tactics for the Wet Fly

Wet flies aren't used much anymore, which is a mistake. They stride the border between nymphs and dry flies. If tied right, with fibrous bodies and hackles soft enough to work in currents, they give an impression of life that most nymphs lack. Because they are fished underwater, not on top, they are able to represent adult insects in a way that dry flies can't.

Most wet flies were devised, and are still fished, to represent winged adult insects, not nymphs or larvae. Once this distinction is apprehended, wets can begin to take the place they once held in our fishing affections. Throughout more than half of our long fly-fishing history, wet flies were the only kind fished. Then they were shouldered aside, first by dry flies, more recently and more brutally by nymphs. But they fill an important niche, and have a place in our fly boxes and our list of fly-fishing tactics.

TYPES OF WET FLIES

Wet flies come in four styles: *traditional winged wets, attractors, wingless wets,* and *soft-hackled wets.* Winged wets were used first on historic English waters. They were imitations of mayfly, caddisfly, and stonefly adults. They were winged because the naturals they imitated had wings.

Attractor wets were devised on this continent when early anglers encountered brook trout. Brookies were foolish enough to take whatever bright flies were thrown at them. The instincts that made them foolish in our eyes helped them survive in their tumbling environment before man came along and ruined it. The brown trout that replaced brookies refused bright flies, and attractor wets are seldom used with much success today.

Wingless wets, or *flymphs,* are similar to traditional wets but lack wings. Most winged wets are tied with stiff quill wings that cleave the water like knife blades. Omitting them often improves the performance of the wet fly. Most people who base their wet-fly selection on natural insects choose wingless wets over traditional, winged wet flies.

Soft-hackle wet flies were developed on the border streams between England and Scotland, and were in use for over 100 years before they were rediscovered by American anglers. Sylvester Nemes, in his 1975 *The Soft-Hackled Fly,* did the rediscovering. It's a delightful book about charming and effective flies.

The three major types of wet flies (from left): traditional winged wet, wingless wet or "flymph," and soft-hackle.

They are, in a way, wingless wets. But their bodies are typically wound of silk threads or floss, and their hackles are of land bird or hen rather than stiffer rooster-neck feathers.

All of my favorite wet-fly patterns are based at least loosely on naturals, not on fancy or whim. Among the winged wets I use the Hare's Ear, Alder, Black Gnat, and Leadwing Coachman, in sizes #10 through #14. All of these represent a variety of insects. In wingless wets I usually carry the Hare's Ear Wingless, Blue Dun Wingless, Little Olive, and Brown Hackle, in #12 through #16. I use soft-hackles more than the others, and depend a lot on the March Brown Spider, Partridge and Yellow, and Partridge and Green, in #10 through #16. This list of wets is spare, but it covers lots of fishing situations.

TACKLE FOR WETS

Tackle for wet-fly fishing is about as simple as it gets. You need a rod, reel, line, leader, and a box of flies. That's about it. Add the nippers and spare tippet material that you need anyway, and you've got what you need. A wet-fly fisherman can travel light.

I don't recommend purchasing any tackle specifically for wet-fly fishing. Other kinds of fishing have more specific needs; what you use for them will work fine for wets. If the rod you carry most of the time is a quick one for fishing small drys, it won't handicap you when tossing wets. If you fish nymphs with indicator and shot, using a longer and slower rod to do it, that also will work fine with wets.

I spend most of my time astream carrying an 8-foot rod balanced for a 5-weight double-taper floating line. It works best with drys. It fishes nymphs well enough, though it could be a foot longer and do a bit better at it. I've never noticed any problems when I switch to wets. If I'm fishing drys and decide to switch, all I do is nip off the dry and tie on the wet.

If I were to select an outfit just for fishing wet flies, the rod would be 7½ to 8 feet long, with a slow to medium action. The line would be the same floating 5-weight double-taper, and the reel would be the smallest and lightest that would hold the line plus 100 yards of backing. The leader would be 9 to 10 feet long, with a 2-foot tippet balanced to the fly size cast.

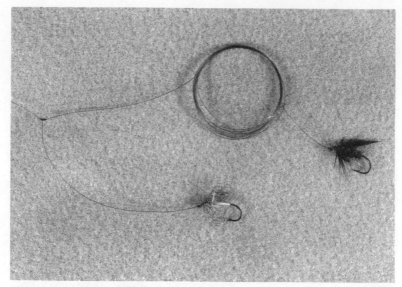

Fishing an extra wet fly on a dropper two or three feet from the point fly lets you try a light fly and a dark one, or a large and small one, to see what the trout prefer.

One old wrinkle in the wet-fly leader has gotten popular again lately. That's the addition of a dropper, so you can fish two flies at the same time. In the early days of American fly fishing most people fished two or three wet flies on a cast. That was the way it was done.

I use droppers on occasion, but not often. They have the advantage of giving the trout a choice between two flies, say a drab one and a bright one, or a large one and small one. It helps you sort out what they want that day. At times a dropper has the added advantage of allowing you to catch two trout on one cast. If you think that's not something considerable, then wait until you've got a couple of fat trout dancing around your ankles. There is a charge to it; I can't deny it.

The easiest way to attach a dropper is to leave the heaviest tag of your tippet knot uncut, and tie the dropper fly to it. Most of the time I try a dropper for a while to find out what is going on, then clip it off along with the tag end of the knot, and fish with the one fly that works best.

INDICATIONS FOR THE WET FLY

A dance of caddis over the water is an indication to fish the wet fly, especially if you try drys first and trout refuse them. Many species of stream caddis swim down to deposit their eggs on the bottom. This usually happens in moderate to fast water, and trout give all the signs of feeding on the surface. Their rises are splashy; they seem greedy. Some of the insects are taken off the top, but more seem to be taken just under the surface.

A mayfly spinner fall is often an indication to fish a sparse wet fly. Lots of spinners are plucked off the surface, but more get drawn under by turbulance, drown, and are taken by trout feeding a few inches below the surface. Wet flies do well when this happens. They are a lot easier to fish at dusk, when spinner falls are common, than dry flies: you can feel the take and don't have to see it when light is low.

Sporadic insect activity of almost any kind is a good indication for fishing wet flies. I've done well with traditional wets or soft-hackle wets when many of the smaller stoneflies are out over the water. Terrestrials are also excellent indications for fishing wets. If you see a few ants in the air, or on rocks and logs alongside the stream, try a Black Gnat in the appropriate size.

Sometimes I turn to wets for the oddest of reasons: they are fun to fish. They don't require paraphernalia attached to your leader; casting is easy. You don't have to watch intently for a strike; you can gaze at the clouds and the birds. They are easy to fish, but they fool lots of trout. That's what makes them fun.

TACTICS FOR WET FLIES

Having said how easy they are to fish, I will also declare that most people don't use wets anymore because they fail to fish them in ways that bring fish to them. The goal, in presenting a wet, is the same as when fishing a dry or nymph: you want to make a fly arrive in front of a fish in a way that a natural might.

Chuck and Chance It

How many times have your heard it? "Don't just throw your flies out there and let the current toss them around. That's just *chuck and chance it."* That's also exactly what nature does with aquatic insects: just throws them out there and lets the currents toss them around. That is why the old method still works so well.

Any wet fly, or brace of them, will work for this kind of fishing. If naturals are in the air, key the fly to them in size, form, and color. You don't need to capture a specimen, though it won't hurt. If you see brown caddis in the air, choose a Hare's Ear, winged or wingless, in the right size. If you see grayish mayfly spinners, then use a sparse Blue Dun Wingless. When you base your fly selection to any degree on prevailing naturals, you already increase your odds beyond pure chance.

The tactic is designed for exploring water: all of it. It's an excellent way to see a stream, get a feel for it, find out where its trout hold. Fish all of the water as you move downstream: riffles, runs, flats, up under the banks, the heads and tails of pools. Don't pass anything up; you never know where a trout will move to the fly.

Take a casting position above and across from whatever bit of

Use the downstream wet fly swing to cover all of the water. Take a couple of steps between casts, so that the fly teases through a new arc of water on each swing.

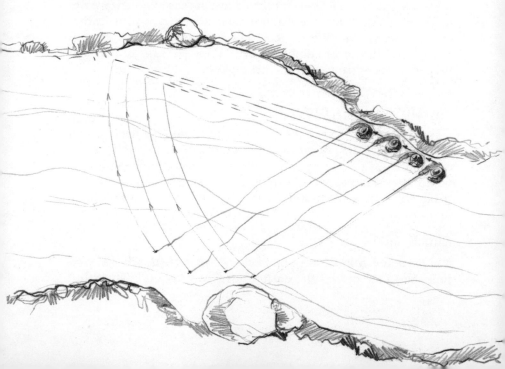

water you intend to cover. Cast at an angle down and across the stream. The acuteness of the angle depends on the speed of the current: the faster the flow, the farther downstream you cast; the slower the flow, the farther upstream you cast.

The goal of the cast is to keep the fly from racing once it lands on the water. It should swing downstream with the current while slowly swimming in toward the bank on your side. Consider what a natural insect, able to swim only feebly, would do in the same water. Then gauge your casting angle so your fly moves at about the same speed. Not many trout will whack a galloping fly, and most of those that do will be small ones.

Hold your rod at about waist height throughout the fly swing and follow the line with the rod tip. This leaves you in the best position to mend line and to set the hook if you feel a fish.

Fish the cast out all the way down and across until it swings into slower water below you. If you wade in slow edge currents and fish into faster water beyond them, then strikes will come most frequently at the moment the fly crosses back over the line between fast water and slow, at the end of the swing.

You can increase the odds further beyond chance by tending the line throughout the drift. If a downstream belly forms, mend the line upstream to slow the fly. Keep mending throughout the drift, if necessary, to pace the swing the way you want it. If the water you fish is slow, then you might want to make a downstream mend in order to install a belly in the line and force the fly to pick up its pace.

I usually fish wets without any action beyond what the current gives them. But I always try some sort of retrieve if the standard drift and swing doesn't produce any action. Most often, this is just a rhythmic raising and lowering of the rod tip, a slight pulse of a few inches that works the fly in short jumps. At times, in slow water, I even try a line-hand retrieve, anywhere from a patient hand twist to a fast strip, leaping the fly along.

Detecting a take, when fishing down and across, is not often difficult. You will feel it. Sometimes the trout raps the fly. Just as often you feel an increasing tension, a weight out there that begins to flap around when you lift your rod to investigate.

To pattern the water with this method, start with short casts at the head of the water you want to fish. Work about two feet of line out on each successive cast. When you have reached the length of line you want to cast, forty to fifty feet, then begin to take a step or two between casts. Work your way downstream this way, so that each swing of the fly covers a fresh arc of water.

Take a few extra casts around any obstruction or obvious holding lie. Let the fly wash around there as much as it will: above the lie, below it, and on both sides. Give the trout lots of chances to see it.

The Soft-hackle Swing

Sylvester Nemes describes this tactic in his book about soft-hackle wets. The tactic itself is based on the greased-line technique developed in Britain for Atlantic salmon fishing. It works well with soft-hackles, but is also excellent when fishing traditional winged and wingless wets.

Your tackle setup should be the standard you use for dry- and wet-fly fishing: a medium to long rod, floating line, and leader the length of the rod or a couple of feet longer. A double-taper line works best for this kind of fishing; line control is at the center of it.

The best water is a riffle or run, at least slightly rumpled, with an even flow from side to side. It should be two to four feet deep, and it helps if there are some features marking the current, indicating rocks and boulders on the bottom. These are scattered holding lies, sheltering trout sprinkled throughout the water.

Take a position at the top end of the water to be fished. Place the cast a few feet upstream from straight across. The first casts should be short, so the fly drifts down the edge of the nearest holding water. The goal is to let the fly drift freely, without influence from line or leader, for about twenty to thirty feet. During this first part of the drift keep your eye on the line, watch for a downstream belly, and mend it before it begins to drag the fly.

Once the fly has reached a position at an angle below you, where you can no longer prevent the line from drawing the fly across stream, then fish out the rest of the swing as you would with a traditional downstream swing. This is not a portion of the drift to neglect. I take most of my trout as the fly swims through this downstream arc.

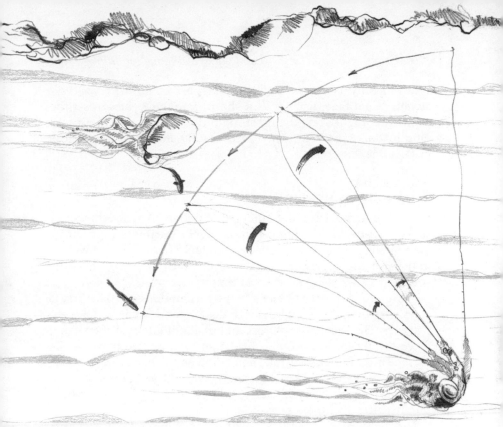

When fishing the soft-hackle swing, mend the line constantly to slow the fly.

Subsequent casts should be made a foot or two farther out in the holding water. Once you cover all of the water you can reach confortably from the first casting position, begin to drop downstream, step and cast, step and cast. But there are disadvantages to covering the water this way. The upper end of the drift, where the fly swims without influence from line and leader, always covers the same lane, because each cast reaches the same distance. It is often better to fish out the water you can reach from one position, then drop down to a new position below the water you've already fished and start with short casts again.

Detecting takes with the soft-hackle swing is easy. Trout that hit in the upper portion of the drift usually make some account of themselves. They rise from the bottom with conviction and turn down so quickly that you can feel the take as a determined tug.

When the fly is on the downstream part of its drift you will always feel a take, usually as a sharp rap. Don't yank to set the hook; you might draw the fly straight upstream out of the trout's mouth. Raise the rod firmly and steadily instead, drawing the hook home.

The Upstream Wet Fly

Wet flies make excellent emerger dressings. A wingless wet or sparse soft-hackle has almost the perfect disarray to represent a mayfly dun trying to escape from its shuck. If you select a wet fly in the size and approximate color of the natural, it will solve the situation a surprising number of times.

There are two ways to fish a wet fly as an emerger. The first is simply to dress the fly lightly with floatant and fish it as if it were a dry fly. The second is to dress all but about a foot of the leader, leave the fly undressed, and fish it an inch or two beneath the surface film. Either way, take a position as close to rising trout as you can get, and make your casts at a slight angle, not straight upstream, so the line and leader fall to the side of the fish while the fly drifts over the top of them.

This tactic is very similar to dry-fly fishing, except that it is much more difficult to follow the drift of the wet fly and to detect takes. If the fly floats in the film, you will see a swirl when a trout takes it. If the fly sinks below the surface you will have to watch where your leader enters the water, or watch your line tip. At any sign of hesitation raise the rod to set the hook gently.

The upstream wet fly also works well on small trout streams and mountain creeks. These are considered dry-fly water, but there are times when trout are shy about drys, usually when the sun is bright and striking down into the water. Since that happens most often in midsummer, when these waters are most fun to explore, and at midday, when they are the most pleasant to fish, I have found more and more days when the wet fly serves me better than the dry on my favorite small waters.

Most wet flies will work on creeks, but I have found wingless wets and soft-hackles best. I tend toward larger sizes, #10 and #12, because trout don't seem to shy away from them and it is easier to see them in the water. For the same reason, I usually use flies with some color, rather than drab dressings. My favorite is the Partridge and Yellow soft-hackle.

The tackle setup is exactly what you would use for dry-fly fishing. Be sure to straighten your leader; any kinks can hurt you because they make it harder to detect takes. It also helps to dress your leader down to within a foot or so of the fly.

Read the water carefully and place the wet wherever you think a trout might hang out. It's fun to use a brace of wets; you can take lots of doubles in small water.

You've got to stalk the water to get into a position close enough so you can see a take to the sunken fly. Use any cover you can crouch behind: boulders, brush, or meadow grasses. Wear clothes that meld into the surroundings of the stream. Stay low, and keep your rod tilted off to the side on the cast.

The cast should be delicate, though I have never noticed that the entry of a fly into the water scares fish on a small creek. Just the opposite: it usually gets their attention and brings them up in a hurry to investigate. I've had them pounce on the fly the second it lands, even when it lands with a thud. But the cast should

When fishing wet flies upstream on small water, you've got to stay out of sight, but be watchful for any sign of a take.

still be delicate so the line and leader don't arrive harshly and frighten the fish. Trout are vulnerable, and therefore spooky, in small water.

Watch the fly if you can see it, or the point where the leader enters the water if you can't. Most of the time you won't even know what tipped you off to a take. You will see some flash of fish, or some mysterious movement of the leader or line. But your arm will raise the rod and set the hook while you're still trying to figure out exactly what told you to do it. Sometimes you never know.

The Leisenring Lift

The Leisenring lift was first recorded in *The Art of Tying the Wet Fly*, in 1941. Pete Hidy coauthored the book with James Leisenring, recording the methods of tying developed by the most famous American wet-fly fisherman. The *lift* was the only fishing tactic detailed in the tying book, and the misconception has grown that it was the only tactic Leisenring used to fish his wet flies. It's far from true.

"Leisenring intended to write a second book," Hidy told me in a conversation not long before he passed away. "It was to detail all of his methods for fishing his wets." The first book was lost in the turmoil that was World War II, and the second book, tragically, was never written. We are left, then, thinking that the Leisenring lift is the way he fished his wets most of the time. It was, in fact, one method in what must have been a full repertoire of wet-fly fishing tactics.

The lift is designed for use in a couple of narrow fishing situations. The first is during a hatch, when trout feed on nymphs or pupae rising toward the surface. The second is over a known or suspected lie when the angler knows exactly where a trout holds, or might hold, and can sink an unweighted fly to the bottom almost in front of the trout's nose.

Leisenring was opposed to any weight on the fly, or on the leader above it. He also stated that he could always catch more trout on the wingless fly, as opposed to the winged wet. A sparse soft-hackle, tied undersized on a stout hook, is just about ideal. The dressing, in size and color, should be based on any prevailing natural. If no insect is predominant use a dressing with which you've had some previous success. I usually fall back on the March Brown Spider or Partridge and Yellow, in #12 or #14, given no outside clues.

Tackle is typical for either dry- or wet-fly fishing: a long rod, double-taper floating line, and a leader a couple of feet longer than the rod. Straighten the leader, but don't dress it with floatant. The tippet should be long, three to four feet, and as fine as you dare make it.

If you are not casting over working trout, then you have to find a lie in water with an even and gentle current: a smooth flow of water leading into the lie so that your fly can sink to it without anything to obstruct it. I don't encounter this kind of lie frequently, which is what leads me to believe strongly that this is just one wet-fly tactic that Leisenring used. He must have had many others adapted to a variety of specific situations.

Once you have pinpointed the trout on the lie you want to fish to, move into position across stream and slightly above it. Working close is not necessary for this method; it works best at between thirty-five and forty-five feet, which lets you stay back and leave your fish undisturbed.

Place the cast several feet above the fish. You will have to use your judgment based on the sink rate of the fly and the speed of the current. The goal is to get the fly down to the level of the trout, or bumping along the bottom. The faster the current the farther upstream you must cast to give the fly a chance to sink. The slower the current the closer you can cast to the trout. The

In the Leisenring Lift, the rod is stopped or lifted just as the fly reaches the position of the trout. This causes the fly to rise toward the surface, just as a natural might.

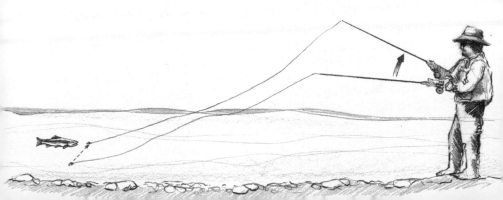

proper lead will usually fall somewhere between five and fifteen feet upstream.

Keep your rod tip high, but follow the drift of the fly as it approaches the lie of the trout. When you see, or feel, that the fly is at the depth of the trout and within a foot or two of its position in the water, then it's time for the *lift*. Stop your rod, keeping it high, and this will stop the line. The fly will suddenly begin to swim toward the surface right in front of the fish. If the lift is executed correctly, few trout can resist it.

There is no reason the Leisenring lift can't be used with nymphs as well as wet flies. When you do, the tactic is very similar to the induced-take nymph technique.

Hidy's Subsurface Swing

During my conversation with the late Pete Hidy, he told me about a tactic he used during hatches. Hidy was not a wet-fly purist, though he was at that time considered the dean of wet-fly fishermen. If trout wanted drys, he fished for them with what they preferred. But if they refused drys, while feeding visibly near the surface, Pete would switch to wets.

He chose a fly based on what he believed the trout were taking. I have found his subsurface swing tactic most useful when adult caddis are dancing around. So many of them lay their eggs by swimming underwater that I always suspect trout of taking adults subsurface when I see a few caddis in the air above the water. So I do my best to capture one and select a wingless wet of similar size and color. Hidy referred to his wingless wets as *flymphs:* the insects they imitated were no longer nymphs, but not yet flies.

The tackle setup is no different than that used for the dry fly. Clip off the dry and tie on the wet. That's all.

The best water type for the method is wherever you find trout rising with visible swirls but refusing dry flies. It might be a riffle or run or even pool, but it needs some current to deliver the fly to the fish, and it works best where visibility is good. I have had the most luck with the subsurface swing on flats and smooth runs.

Move into position above the rising trout and across from it. Make the cast down and across stream to the working fish, plac-

Hidy's Subsurface Swing is employed on fish holding high in the water. The fly is given a tug to pop it underwater, then allowed to swing across the position of the trout.

ing the fly about two feet above it and two feet beyond it. Because the wingless wet is fibrous, it will normally float for a bit on top of the water. Hidy instructed me to give it a slight tug to pull it beneath the surface. "When it is fished this way," he said, "the flymph entrains tiny bubbles of air in its fibers, and looks exactly like the natural swimming underwater."

Once the fly has been pulled under, then let the current swing it down and draw it across, in front of the rising trout. In my experience, takes come satisfyingly often and you have no trouble detecting them. You can see the swirl, and you can feel the determined pull of a satisfied fish.

One that has been completely fooled.

9

Fishing the Streamer

Ray Bergman said it first in his biblical *Trout:* Too many people use streamers only when the water is high and cloudy. The rest of the time, which usually means most of the season after spring runoff, the streamer wallet is tucked away and forgotten.

I take more trout on streamers when the water is low and clear than I do when it is high and cloudy. But this reflects a preference to fish water that has dropped into what I consider fishable condition. Streamers are excellent for covering lots of different water types in a disciplined hurry, whether the water is in shape or out of it. Streamers and bucktails represent a variety of baitfish that are present and active no matter what condition the water is in. They are an excellent way to find interested trout.

An indistinct but discernible division occurs between baitfish in the East and the West. Most eastern types are species of dace, or similar to them. They have a slender minnowlike form, with flashing silver sides as they dart about in shallows and back-waters. Most western types are sculpin species, with blocky bull-head shapes and mottled camouflage colors. They live cryptically among the bottom stones in riffles and runs, exposing themselves to trout only when they make a short dash to a new hiding spot on the bottom.

Trout fry are overlooked but essential candidates for streamer imitations, East and West. They are often present in great numbers, and are in constant danger because they hover along the edges of the exact habitat they will move into later when they grow a bit. Brown trout are the most notorious cannibals of smaller trout, but they have gained that reputation simply because their inherent caution allows more of them to reach sufficient size to turn on their own kind. Given equal size a brook trout, cutthroat, or even a rainbow will nip off a fry.

Leeches aren't exactly baitfish, but they are one of the best trout foods to imitate with streamers. Their large size, abundance in some waters, and undulating movement make them available and enticing to trout.

Traditional feather-winged streamers such as the Gray Ghost are complicated but beautiful dressings. Most of them are tied to imitate baitfish found in lakes. Bucktails such as the Black-Nose Dace, Mickey Finn, and Royal Coachman Bucktail are easier to tie, and more useful as imitations of trout-stream baitfish. The Little Brown Trout, Little Rainbow Trout, and Little Brook Trout streamers should fish well in almost any trout waters. It is helpful, but not always necessary, to choose the dressing that corresponds to the species your waters hold.

The Royal Coachman Bucktail, Muddler Minnow, and Woolly Bugger are typical of the various streamer types.

The Muddler Minnow imitates sculpins. It is the most popular streamer on western waters. Marabou dressings such as Olive or Black Woolly Buggers and the Black Marabou Muddler have the right action to imitate lots of things, leeches chief among them. The wavy action of marabou catches every tendril of current; these flies come alive even when fished without any action added by the angler.

Streamers are tied on hooks from size #2/0 down to #12. On big western waters they are used from #2/0 to #6. In the East smaller sizes seem more typical, from #8 to #12. Most traditional streamers are tied without weight. They fish well in thin water, where any weight would deliver them to the bottom far too quickly. If desired, they can be taken down with a wet-tip line, or with a single split shot pinched to the leader at the fly head. Marabou streamers are usually tied with some weight added to the hook shank.

Quite a few different retrieves can be useful when fishing streamers. They are based on the way natural foods move in the water.

The most effective retrieve is often no retrieve at all. Allow the streamer to fish as it will, activated by the currents. This is done most often with the traditional downstream swing, in which the fly fishes out its drift without manipulation from the rod or the line hand. But it also works when you fish a streamer down on the bottom of a big western riffle or run, letting it tumble along freely like a baitfish no longer in control of its own destiny.

A rhythmic pulse of the rod tip, while the fly accomplishes its swing on a tight line, adds a darting motion to the fly. The action can be added without gathering line, so that the fly seems to alternately swim forward, then rest. Raise and lower the rod about a foot at the most. It is often more effective to twitch the rod tip just a few inches in a quick repeated pulse.

The most popular streamer retrieve is the short strip. Hold the line under the forefinger of the rod hand. Draw in line with quick strips of the line hand, anywhere from 4 to 12 inches at a time. The fly darts forward, as it does on the pulsing retrieve, then rests. But this method also draws the fly through the water, rather than letting it swing through a normal arc. Combined with mends and flips of your line, it can be used to swim the fly over and around and through a boulder field in a moderate or slow run. This is big-fish habitat, and one of the best places to fish a streamer.

The strip-and-twitch retrieve combines short strips with a constant rhythmic twitching of the rod tip. This darts the fly nervously throughout its entire swing or retrieve. It works best in moderate to slow water, where the streamer would not have much life of its own when left to the whim of the current.

A long stripping retrieve gives the impression of a baitfish fleeing, which is what naturals do when chased by trout. If you fish fast water, then the current tends to give the fly this natural speed. In slower water a fast retrieve can give the impression of fear to your fly, and add some incentive to a big trout's chase. Ernest Schwiebert, in his masterful *Trout,* called this the *panic strip.*

All combinations and permutations of these basic retrieves, and any others you might make up on the spot, can be effective at certain times. It always helps to vary your retrieve. Experiment with different speeds and depths more than you experiment with fly patterns. We often make the mistake of changing flies when a change in the way we fish the same fly would make more difference.

TACKLE FOR FISHING STREAMERS

Tackle for streamer fishing seems at first glance to be specialty gear, heavy stuff. But think a bit before you trot back to the car to change rods. Most streamers should be at least slightly in keeping with the size water you fish. If you are on a tiny stream, then your streamers shouldn't be much bigger than wet flies, #10 and #12. They shouldn't tax your light gear. If you're on a medium-sized trout stream, using an 8- to 9-foot rod that casts a 5- or 6-weight line, then the streamers you use, sizes #6 through #10, should be no problem to cast if you make sure the leader balances them.

If you're on a big western river, and want to belt out #2/0 to #4 streamers, heavily weighted, then go on and trot. Get your heavy rod. You'll wear yourself out casting bombs with your light or your medium rod. If you're fishing from a boat, you'll wear out your welcome by pelting everybody else with them.

If you decide to gear up specifically for streamer fishing, the rod should be long, 8½ feet or longer. Its action should be slow to medium for relatively open, patient loops. The reel for streamer fishing should hold the line plus at least 100 yards of backing, and should have a reliable drag.

The line should be a floater. Streamer fishing is one of the rare kinds where I recommend the weight-forward taper, not as much for long casts as for the extra heft out toward the end of the line, to boss the fly around. The double-taper gives more line control on the water, and line control can be extremely important in streamer fishing. It's a trade-off; I'd use a weight-forward if the outfit was strictly for streamers. Carry a spare spool with a weight-forward wet-tip with a fast sink rate, to help get the fly down when you don't want to weight it.

The leader should be eight to ten feet long, and should have its tapers stacked toward the heavy end. If the butt diameters are thin the leader will not transfer all the energy of the line down to the fly, and your cast will crumple. So much streamer fishing is done toward the banks, or toward specific holding lies, that a collapsed leader results in a wasted cast.

TACTICS FOR STREAMERS

The Traditional Streamer Swing

Traditional streamer fishing is a lot like the traditional downstream wet-fly swing. It works for a lot of the same reasons. It shows an imitation of a baitfish in a realistic fashion over lots of water, to lots of trout. It is excellent for exploring water.

The best water type for the tactic is any part of the stream that has a marked flow, from slow to dashing. It works well in riffles, runs, and all parts of pools, and on broad flats.

Because you will be wading downstream as you fish, take your initial position at the head of the water to be fished. Wade in far enough upstream that the first fly swing carries through the water farthest upstream that you think might hold trout. As with other kinds of fishing requiring casts down and across the stream, the most common problem is wading right into water at the very head of a riffle, run, or pool where you should be fishing.

The angle of the cast is determined by the speed of the current.

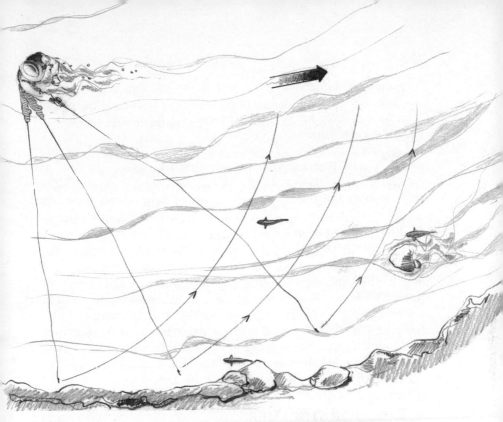

When fishing the downstream streamer swing, lengthen the casts so that each covers a new arc of water. When you've fished all that you can reach from the first position, move downstream and cover a fresh area of water, or else step-and-cast down the pool.

The faster the water, the farther you must cast downstream to reduce the speed of the swing. The slower the current, the higher upstream the cast is made. In very slow water the cast can be made straight across; it's often helpful to mend a downstream belly into the line in order to speed the swing of the fly, not slow it, in currents that creep along.

It is always helpful to give the fly a few feet of drift to sink. The object is not to get the fly down to the bottom, but to keep it from breaking back up through the surface, where it would leave a wake. At times, in water more than about four feet deep, it's best to get the fly down at least a couple of feet. This is best accomplished by switching to a wet-tip line, but you can also pinch a split shot on the leader adjacent to the fly eye.

When the streamer has reached the depth you want, let the current pick up the line and begin to swing it around. Follow it with the rod tip, holding the rod low to give maximum leverage if a trout strikes.

Gauge the speed of the streamer the same as you do with the wet-fly swing: the objective is to swim the fly across and downstream, in an arc, at about the same speed a baitfish might swim. If the fly begins to move too fast, use upstream mends to slow it down. If it pokes along, use downstream mends to put a belly in the line and pick up the speed of the fly.

The current often gives the fly all of the action it needs in the standard streamer swing. But there are times when the addition of some life with the rod tip or line hand perks up the interest of trout. The easiest way to add action is to lift and lower the rod in a steady rhythmic pulse. You can add short strips with the line hand, or use the strip and twitch, which causes the fly to stutter along enticingly. It never hurts to experiment; sometimes it even helps to use more than one type of retrieve on the same cast.

Let the fly swing all the way around below you. If you are wading at the edge of a riffle, make sure the streamer crosses the seam between fast and slow water before you pick it up. Let it hang there, or even give it some action, working it up into the current, then letting it settle back down. Never be in a hurry to lift a streamer out of the water. Trout often follow for several feet before deciding to rush in for the take.

The traditional streamer swing is an excellent method for covering lots of water. Move downstream, taking a couple of steps between casts, fishing the streamer on its constant arcs, making sure to work it in and around any visible boulders, seams, and ledges. But fish all of the water, even where it seems too shallow to hold a trout. Large fish often forage into thin water, and they are after baitfish when they do. A streamer swimming by can make a V-wake well up behind it. Hold on!

The Cross-stream Streamer.

This method is similar to the standard downstream swing, but works best in slow water, or in water where you want to get your streamer down near the bottom. Again, if you want depth switch to a wet-tip line before beginning to fish, or pinch a shot above the eye of the streamer.

The cross-stream cast works well for fishing the kind of shelving water that is deepest along the far bank. It is effective for probing undercut banks. You want your fly to fish through the deep water, and are not so concerned about the rest of the swing, as the water gradually becomes shallower toward your bank. But it's always wise to fish out the cast. You never know when a trout might follow the fly out of deep water and pounce when it looks like it is about to escape into the shallows.

Your casting position should be straight across from the water to be fished. The cast should be made at an angle a few feet upstream. This gives the fly a chance to sink before it reaches a

When fishing a streamer on cross-stream casts to a deep bank, mend line to keep the fly in deep water as long as you can.

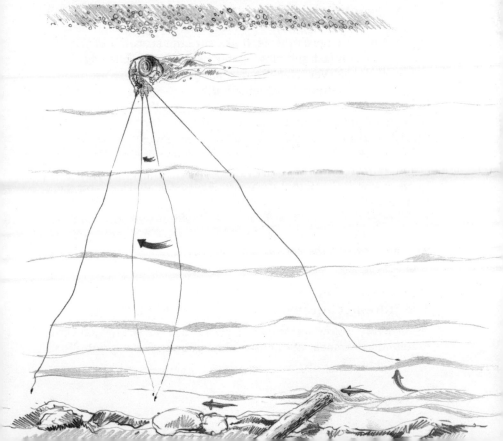

holding lie. The distance upstream depends on the depth of the water and the speed of the current. If it's only three to four feet deep, with a slow current, five feet might be enough. If the water is six to eight feet deep, or the current fairly fast, then you might need to cast as far as twenty feet upstream from the water where you want the streamer to reach fishing depth.

The upper portion of the drift is designed to let the fly sink. The line should come tight against the fly, and you should be ready to begin fishing out the cast, at about the time it reaches a point straight across from you. At that point you need to have the line angling as straight toward the fly as you can get it. That will often require an upstream mend or two.

The goal is to get the fly to swim slowly across the deeper part of the water, but also to keep the fly in that deep water as long as you can. This sometimes requires almost constant mending and tending of the line, although in some currents the fly rides exactly where you want it without any direction at all.

A dead drift works well on this kind of cast. Keep just enough tension against the fly so you can feel a hit if it happens. Then let the fly ride along with the current. The slight tension of the line will keep the fly in a swimming posture, as if it's just lazing along. You can also add action with a slight pulsing of the rod. If the deep water extends toward your bank, then a stripping retrieve can be used to swim the streamer through a downstream swing back to a position straight below you.

It is always wise to fish out the complete swing, even after the fly moves out of deep water, in case a fish is following it. You can speed up this part of the drift, if you'd like, with a panic strip. It might goose a fish into a decision. At least it will get you back into position for your next cast quickly.

To cover the water in a disciplined fashion with this method, just drop downstream a couple of steps between casts. Each cast will then sweep the fly on a new drift line through the deep water.

The Stillwater Streamer

Not every river has stillwater pools. But those that do have excellent streamer water because lots of baitfish hang out where the water isn't pushy. If the water is deep, or has cover for holding lies, big trout like the same kind of water.

Tackle for this kind of fishing depends on the size of the river. If it is small to medium water, then your light to medium rod will fish it well enough. You wouldn't want to switch. If the water is big, however, you will probably want your heavy rod. Long casts help you cover more water. And you will often find it necessary to wade deep, giving the long rod an advantage.

Use your wet-tip line, or a floater, on smaller water. For the biggest rivers, it is sometimes helpful to fish with a Hi-Density Shooting Head, but rigging for a head is somewhat complicated, and you wouldn't want to make a switch unless you had a reel set up specifically for fishing with heads. If you fish a lot of big water, though, it pays to take time to rig such a setup, with running line and backing already in place.

Your position should be anywhere on the rim of the pool that lets you reach the water you want to fish. Given an option, it would be best to start at the upper end of the water and fish it downstream.

The cast should be made just upstream from straight across. If there is a current this gives the fly a chance to sink before you begin your retrieve. If there is little or no current, cast in a pattern that lets you cover all of the water you can reach from each position, then move to a new one, as you might fish a small pond.

Give the fly lots of time to sink. Trout rarely hold anywhere but right on the bottom in still water, unless they feed actively or hunt the shallows. If they are on the bottom they are seldom willing to move very high up in the water column to take a fly. Get down deep. Weighted flies are excellent for fishing still water; you might want to pinch a shot above the fly if it is unweighted.

Once the fly has gotten down to where you want it, begin your retrieve. All sorts of retrieves are effective, but I have had my best luck on a hand twist, or a very slow strip, combined with a rhythmic twitching of the rod tip.

Fishing a still pool is a bit like fishing a pond: experiment with fly pattern, depth fished, and speed of retrieve until you find a combination the trout want. Usually, for me, the fly pattern is a

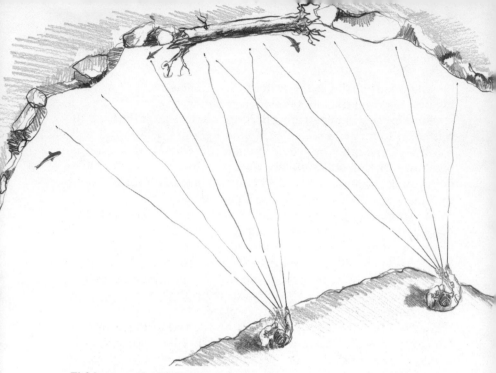

Fishing a pool with little current requires casting in fan-shaped arcs from each position to cover all the water.

Woolly Bugger or Muddler, the depth the bottom, and the speed slow. But there are times when trout will squirt almost to the top to intercept a streamer that is galloped.

Cover all the water, from the head to the tail-shallows. Probe most carefully along undercut banks, around obstructions, and down in the dark depths at the center of the pool.

Fishing Streamers from a Boat

If you fish from a boat it's got to be on medium to big water or it wouldn't float you. The best way to fish such water is to drift along and hit the salient features as you come to them – more often as they whiz past you.

Use weighted flies for this kind of fishing: you want them to start sinking the second they hit the water. For the largest rivers the flies are often very large and heavily weighted. They are tough to cast, but your heavy rod will take at least some of the pain out of it. If you use your light or even your medium rod, scale your flies down to suit the outfit or plan to get lumps on the back of your head.

Nothing says you can't fish the banks from a boat with flies of modest size. I do most of mine with Woolly Buggers and Marabou Muddlers in #6 and #8. They are weighted with ten to fifteen turns of lead wire the diameter of the hook shank. When fishing these modest flies from a boat I usually use my medium outfit. It's 8½ feet long, graphite, and casts a weight-forward 7-weight line. It is slightly fast for the job, but it's what I own, and I like its action for most of the things I use my medium to do. I would, in truth, rather fish this medium and the smaller streamers than fish the heavy rod and the larger streamers that are usually used when floating big western waters. But I'll confess that lots of people use stout gear and #2 flies to take fish that outweigh mine.

You've got to keep looking in two directions at once in this kind of fishing. Most of your attention should be focused on the water coming up: read it for boulders and other obvious holding lies, and watch the banks for indentations, rocks, and anything else that breaks the current and forms a potential holding lie. The rest

Fishing a streamer to the banks will let you lead a lot of nice trout to your boat.

of your attention should be paid to the cast you are currently making, or fishing out.

Things happen quickly when you fish from a moving boat. The next lie you want to hit rushes at you, the last cast you've made has just landed; perhaps you've felt a slight thump as it sank, and wish you could let the fly trail in the water a little longer in hopes the fish will hit again. But you know it would be better to pick the fly up, make a quick backcast, and place it back where the thump happened, or get on to the next lie. There are almost always three things you should be doing at once in boat fishing a fast river, which means you are going to do at least one of them wrong.

The best thing to do is relax and hit what holding lies you can without haste. A hasty backcast is one of the forbiddens in boat fishing: it is what causes clients to whack themselves, and their guides, with weighted flies. Even the best fisherman, with the best gear, can't make things happen the way they should happen and still make them happen in a hurry. Slow down. You can even look up at the scenery once in a while; tell your guide I said it was all right.

Take your lies one at a time, whether they are boulders lying out in the current or pockets lying against the banks. Calculate your cast so that the fly will land just before the boat reaches a position straight across from the lie. Let the fly sink while the boat passes the holding water, then draw the line tight, make a few strips with your line hand, and keep the rod low so you can set the hook if you feel a strike.

When you've fished the fly out five to ten feet from the lie, pick it up and cast again. You might be able to probe the same lie with one more long cast, or your eye might have already picked out the next lie, and your next cast should go to it.

You can also fish streamers from a boat exactly the same way you fish heavily weighted nymphs. Make the cast at an angle behind the boat, give the fly a few seconds to sink, then tighten against it and make a short retrieve. If nothing happens pick up and make your next cast.

The boat, which floats in faster current than the fly at the bank, helps to draw the line tight, which makes it easier to tell when you've had a hit. There will be times, when fishing this way, that your line tip takes a jump just after the fly hits the water. When this happens it's an indication that a fish has boiled out, taken your fly, and turned back to its lie with it. Always fish with your rod held low in this kind of fishing; you want to be able to raise the rod and set the hook hard the instant you see some subtle sign of a take.

Most often, though, your takes to streamers will be hard, almost brutal. You won't have to wonder what has happened. You won't even have to set the hook.

The trout will do that for you.

Conclusion:
The Tactic of Change

When you think of tactics for trout, there are lots of options to call on. But there are usually some hints within a situation that help you decide which method might work best: a hatch of mayfly duns on a broad flat, a dance of caddis in sunshine over a bright riffle, or even the absence of indications which in itself tells you a lot about what to do and what kinds of flies to do it with.

There are four main aspects to trout-stream fishing: learning to read water and find fish, gaining some knowledge of trout foods in order to select appropriate fly patterns, selecting balanced tackle and mastering casting techniques, and finally developing a battery of useful tactics to take the trout.

There is an additional element that makes all the others more effective. That is *change*. You've got to be constantly aware of the need to change as the situation demands it. That will be often throughout the course of an average fishing day. The biggest mistake made by beginning fly fishermen, and lots of experienced ones as well, is failure to observe what is happening and then responding to it.

Change, as an element of fly fishing, follows a logical pro-
gression.

If you fish over trout, or over water you think should hold
trout, and don't have any luck, then the first thing to change is
your presentation. Change the way you show the fly to the trout:
move to a different position, try a different kind of cast, or a
different kind of retrieve.

The next thing to change is the fly itself. If trout disdain what
you're using, look at your sources again: what natural are the
trout taking? What imitation are they likely to take? This might
mean switching to a more imitative fly in a selective situation; it
might merely mean changing to a drabber fly because the day is
bright, or a smaller fly because trout move toward your fly but
turn shy of taking it.

If changing fly patterns doesn't inspire the trout, change fly
types. Give up drys and go to nymphs, wets, or streamers. It can
just as easily be reversed: if trout refuse sunken flies, try them
up top.

If changing fly styles doesn't work, change the level at which
you fish. I don't know how many times in nymph fishing an
added split shot has made the difference between no fish at all
and fish that were suddenly abundant. They had been there all
along, probably no more than a foot or two below the drift of my
fly. At times an extra mend can accomplish the same thing when
you fish wets or streamers, getting the fly down deeper.

If all else fails, change the water type you fish. It's great to
hover around a flat all day, waiting for trout to start rising – *if*
they start rising. But the hatch might fail you entirely. Move to a
riffle or run, and catch some trout while you wait. If you're on
foot and on a small to medium stream, then hike for a while, see
some water, try some different water types. Don't just hang
around and wait for something to happen where you stand. If
you're in a boat, pull up the anchor, drift some distance, look for
some action.

Finally, if none of the other changes work, try changing
streams. This isn't always possible, but if you're on a trip, and the
stream you've driven miles to fish isn't producing – because of
high water, lack of hatches, too many people, whatever – move
out. Try another stream.

Trout are always biting somewhere.

Appendix A
Dry Flies

SEARCHING DRIES

Elk Hair Caddis
Hook: Standard dry fly, #10–#16
Thread: Tan 6/0
Rib: Gold wire, counterwound through hackle
Body: Tan fur or synthetic
Hackle: Ginger
Wing: Tan elk hair

Deer Hair Caddis
Hook: Standard dry fly, #10–#16
Thread: Gray 6/0
Body: Olive fur or synthetic
Hackle: Blue dun
Wing: Natural dun deer hair

Dry flies. Row 1 (left to right): **Elk Hair Caddis, Deer Hair Caddis, Adams, Light Cahill, Blue-winged Olive.** Row 2: **Royal Coachman, Beetle Bug, Royal Wulff, Humpy.** Row 3: **Pale Morning Compara-dun, Little Olive Compara-dun, Little Olive Emerger, Rusty Compara-spinner, Quill-winged Caddis.** Row 4: **Fluttering Caddis, Langtry Special, Stimulator, Griffith's Gnat, Adams Midge.** Row 5: **Black Feather Beetle, Black Ant, Letort Hopper, Letort Cricket.** *Andrew E. Cier*

Adams
Hook: Standard dry fly, #12–#16
Thread: Black 6/0
Wings: Grizzly hackle tips
Tail: Grizzly and brown hackle, mixed
Body: Muskrat fur
Hackle: Grizzly and brown, mixed

Light Cahill
Hook: Standard dry fly, #12–#16
Thread: Tan 6/0
Wings: Wood-duck flank, upright and divided
Tail: Light ginger hackle
Body: Cream badger underfur or synthetic
Hackle: Light ginger

Blue-Winged Olive
Hook: Standard dry fly, #12–#16
Thread: Olive 6/0
Wings: Dark blue-dun hackle tips
Tail: Dark blue-dun hackle
Body: Brownish olive fur
Hackle: Dark blue dun

Royal Coachman
Hook: Standard dry fly, #10–#16
Thread: Black 6/0
Wings: White mallard quill
Tail: Golden pheasant tippets
Body: Peacock herl/red floss/peacock herl
Hackle: Coachman brown

Beetle Bug
Hook: Standard dry fly, #10–#14
Thread: Black 6/0
Wings: White calf body hair
Tail: Moose body fibers
Body: Fluorescent red fur
Hackle: Coachman brown

Royal Wulff
Hook: Standard dry fly, #8–#14
Thread: Black 6/0
Wing: White calf tail
Tail: Moose body fibers
Body: Peacock herl/red floss/peacock herl
Hackle: Coachman brown

Humpy
Hook: Standard dry fly, #8–#14
Thread: Yellow 6/0
Tail: Moose body hair
Underbody: Yellow thread
Overbody: Moose body hair
Wing: Deer-hair tips
Hackle: Grizzly and brown, mixed

IMITATIVE DRIES

Pale Morning Compara-dun
Hook: 1XF (extra fine) dry fly, #16–#18
Thread: Pale yellow 6/0
Wing: Cream deer hair
Tails: Ginger hackle fibers, split
Body: Yellow-olive fur or synthetic

Little Olive Compara-dun
Hook: 1XF dry fly, #16–#20
Thread: Olive 6/0
Wing: Natural dun deer hair
Tails: Blue-dun hackle fibers, split
Body: Olive fur or synthetic

Little Olive Emerger
Hook: 1XF dry fly, #14–#18
Thread: Olive 6/0
Tails: Blue dun hackle fibers, split
Body: Brownish olive fur
Wing clump: Knot of gray polypro yarn
Legs: Blue dun hackle fibers

Rusty Compara-spinner
Hook: 1XF dry fly, #12–#16
Thread: Brown 6/0
Tails: Brown hackle fibers, split
Body: Reddish brown fur or synthetic
Wings: Brown hackle, clipped top and bottom

Quill-Winged Caddis
Hook: 1XF dry fly, #10–#16
Thread: Gray 6/0
Body: Light olive fur or synthetic
Wing: Turkey quill
Hackle: Dark ginger

Fluttering Caddis
Hook: 1XF dry fly, #10–#16
Thread: Black
Body: Olive-brown fur or synthetic
Wing: Gray mink tail guard fibers
Hackle: Dark blue dun

Langtry Special
Hook: 3XL, #6–#8
Thread: Orange 6/0
Tail: Tan elk hair
Aft Hackle: Brown, palmered over abdomen
Abdomen: Cream fur or synthetic
Wing: Tan elk hair
Fore Hackle: Brown, palmered over thorax
Thorax: Orange fur or synthetic

Stimulator
Hook: 3XL, #6–#10
Thread: Orange 6/0
Tail: Deer body hair
Rib: Grizzly hackle, palmered
Abdomen: Yellow fur
Wing: Deer body hair
Hackle: Grizzly, palmered over thorax
Thorax: Orange fur

Griffith's Gnat
Hook: 1XF dry fly, #16–#24
Thread: Black 6/0
Hackle: Grizzly, palmered over body
Body: Peacock herl

Adams Midge
Hook: 1XF dry fly, #16–#22
Thread: Black 6/0
Tail: Grizzly hackle fibers
Body: Muskrat fur
Hackle: Grizzly

Black Feather Beetle
Hook: 1XF dry fly, #12–#20
Thread: Black 6/0
Body: Peacock herl
Hackle: Black, palmered, trimmed top and bottom
Wing: Two feathers from ringneck collar, trimmed to shape

Black Ant
Hook: 1XF dry fly, #14–#18
Thread: Black 6/0
Abdomen: Black fur or synthetic
Hackle: Black, 2–3 turns only
Thorax: Black fur or synthetic

Letort Hopper
Hook: 2XL, #10–#14
Thread: Yellow 6/0
Body: Yellow fur or synthetic
Underwing: Mottled turkey quill
Overwing: Deer body hair
Head: Spun and clipped butts of overwing

Letort Cricket
Hook: 2XL, #10–#14
Thread: Black 6/0
Body: Black fur or synthetic
Underwing: Black goose quill
Overwing: Black deer body hair
Head: Spun and clipped butts of overwing

Appendix B: Nymphs

SEARCHING NYMPHS

Gold-Ribbed Hare's Ear
Hook: 1XL, extra stout, #8–#16
Thread: Black 6/0
Weight: 8–12 turns lead wire
Tail: Tuft of hare's poll fur
Rib: Narrow gold tinsel
Abdomen: Tan fur from hare's mask
Wing Case: Brown mottled turkey
Thorax: Darker fur from hare's mask

Zug Bug
Hook 1XL, extra stout, #8–#16
Thread: Black 6/0
Weight: 8–12 turns lead wire
Tail: Peacock sword
Rib: Oval silver tinsel
Body: Peacock herl
Hackle: Furnace, sparse
Wing Case: Wood-duck flank, clipped short

Nymphs. Row 1 (left to right): Gold-Ribbed Hare's Ear, Zug Bug, Muskrat, Girdle Bug. Row 2: Bitch Creek Nymph, Pheasant Tail, Green Caddis Larva, Brown and Yellow Deep Pupa. Row 3: Brown and Bright Green Deep Pupa, Dark Gray Pupa, Ginger Deep Pupa, Montana Stone, Box Canyon Stone. Row 4: Traditional Midge Pupa, Lees Ferry Shrimp, Olive Scud, Near Enough, Black Drake. *Andrew F. Cier*

Muskrat
Hook: 3XL, #8–#16
Thread: Black
Body: Muskrat fur twisted in dubbing noodle
Legs: Guinea feather fibers
Head: Black ostrich herl

Girdle Bug
Hook: 3XL, #4–#8
Thread: Black
Weight: 15–25 turns lead wire
Tail: White rubber hackle
Body: Black chenille
Legs: White rubber hackle

Bitch Creek Nymph
Hook: 3XL, #4–#8
Thread: Black
Weight: 15–25 turns lead wire
Tail: White rubber hackle
Abdomen: Black and orange chenille, woven
Hackle: Brown, palmered over thorax
Thorax: Black chenille
Antennae: White rubber hackle

IMITATIVE NYMPHS

Pheasant Tail
Hook: Standard dry fly, #12–#18
Thread: Brown 6/0
Tail: Ringneck tail fibers
Rib: Gold wire, counterwound
Body: Ringneck tail fibers, as herl
Legs: Ringneck tail-fiber butts

Green Caddis Larva
Hook: English bait hook, #10–#14
Thread: Black
Weight: 8–12 turns lead wire
Abdomen: Green fur or synthetic
Legs: Mottled grouse
Thorax: Brown fur or synthetic

Brown and Yellow Deep Pupa
Hook: Standard dry fly, #12–#16
Thread: Brown 6/0
Weight: 8–12 turns lead or copper wire
Underbody: One-half russet or gold Sparkle Yarn, one-half
    brown fur, mixed and dubbed
Overbody: Russet or gold Sparkle Yarn
Hackle: Lemon wood-duck fibers along lower half of sides
Head: Brown marabou strands or brown fur

Brown and Bright Green Deep Pupa
Hook: Standard dry fly, #12–#16
Thread: Brown 6/0
Weight: 8–12 turns lead or copper wire
Underbody: One-third olive Sparkle Yarn, two-thirds bright green acrylic craft fur, mixed and dubbed
Overbody: Medium olive Sparkle Yarn
Hackle: Dark grouse fibers along lower half of sides
Head: Brown marabou strands or brown fur

Dark Gray Deep Pupa
Hook: Standard dry fly, #12–#16
Thread: Gray 6/0
Weight: 8–12 turns lead or copper wire
Underbody: One-half medium gray fur, one-half dark brown Sparkle Yarn, mixed and dubbed
Overbody: Gray Sparkle Yarn
Hackle: Dark gray hen-hackle fibers along lower half of sides
Head: Dark gray marabou fibers or dark gray fur

Ginger Deep Pupa
Hook: Standard dry fly, #12–#16
Thread: Tan 6/0
Weight: 8–12 turns copper or lead wire
Underbody: One-half cream fur, one-half amber Sparkle Yarn, mixed and dubbed
Overbody: Amber Sparkle Yarn
Hackle: Lemon wood-duck fibers along lower half of sides
Head: Cream marabou fibers or cream fur

Montana Stone
Hook: 3XL, #4–#8
Thread: Black
Weight: 20–25 turns lead wire
Tail: Raven or crow primary, split
Rib: Brown flat monofilament
Body: Black fuzzy yarn
Hackle: Grizzly and brown (stripped on one side)
Gills: White ostrich herl, tied in with hackle

Box Canyon Stone
Hook: 3XL, #4–#8
Thread: Black
Weight: 15–25 turns lead wire
Tails: Goose quill fibers, split
Abdomen: Black yarn
Wing Case: Mottled turkey quill
Hackle: Furnace, palmered over thorax
Thorax: Black yarn

Traditional Midge Pupa
Hook: Standard dry fly, #12–#20
Thread: Match body color, 6/0
Swimmers and gill tufts: White polypro yarn laid along hook
  shank, clipped at tail and head
Rib: Silver wire
Body: Fur to match natural (black, tan, and olive are most com-
  mon)

Lees Ferry Shrimp
Hook: 1XL, extra stout, #10–#14
Thread: Beige 3/0 Monocord
Weight: 12–15 turns .015 or .017 lead wire
Rib: Working thread
Tail and shellback: Tan elk hair
Body and legs: Two-thirds beige Sparkle Yarn blended with one-
  third #30 Flyrite for tan shrimp, with one-third #23 Flyrite for
  olive shrimp
Head: Trimmed shellback butts

Olive Scud
Hook: 1XL, extra stout, #12–#16
Thread: Olive 6/0
Weight: 8–12 turns fine lead wire
Tail: Olive hackle fibers
Shellback: Clear plastic from freezer bag
Rib: Olive thread
Body: Olive-gray seal fur mixed with olive rabbit fur
Legs: Olive hackle fibers
Antennae: Wood-duck flank fibers

Near Enough
Hook: 3XL, #8–#14
Thread: Tan
Tail: Mallard flank fibers, dyed tan
Body: Gray fox fur
Legs: Mallard flank fibers, dyed tan
Wing Case: Butts of leg fibers

Black Drake
Hook: 3XL, #10–#14
Thread: Gray
Tail: Speckled guinea fibers
Body: Beaver belly fur
Legs: Speckled guinea fibers
Wing Case: Black ostrich flues

Appendix C:
Wet Flies

TRADITIONAL WINGED WETS

Hare's Ear
Hook: Standard dry fly, #10-#14
Thread: Black 6/0
Tail: Brown hackle fibers
Rib: Narrow gold tinsel
Body: Hare's ear fur, with guard hairs
Wing: Hen pheasant wing quill

Alder
Hook: Standard dry fly, #10-#14
Thread: Black 6/0
Body: Peacock herl
Hackle: Black hen
Wing: Mottled turkey quill

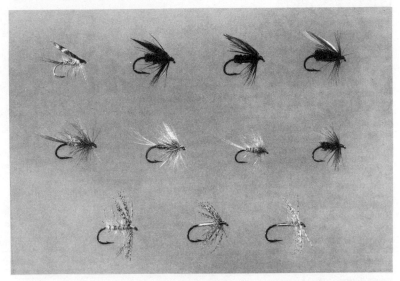

Wet flies. Row 1 (left to right): Hare's Ear, Alder, Black Gnat, Leadwing Coachman. Row 2: Hare's Ear Wingless, Blue Dun Wingless, Little Olive Flymph, Brown Hackle. Row 3: March Brown Spider, Partridge and Yellow, Partridge and Green. *Andrew E. Cier*

Black Gnat
Hook: Standard dry fly, #10-#14
Thread: Black 6/0
Body: Black chenille
Hackle: Black hen
Wing: Goose or mallard wing quill

Leadwing Coachman
Hook: Standard dry fly, #10–#14
Thread: Black
Tag: Medium gold tinsel
Body: Peacock herl
Hackle: Coachman brown hen
Wing: Mallard wing quill

WINGLESS WETS

Hare's Ear Wingless
Hook: Standard dry fly, #10–#16
Thread: Brown 6/0
Tail: Brown hackle fibers
Rib: Narrow gold tinsel
Body: Hare's mask fur
Hackle: Brown hen

Blue Dun Wingless
Hook: Standard dry fly, #10–#16
Thread: Gray 6/0
Tail: Blue-dun hen-hackle fibers
Rib: Narrow gold tinsel
Body: Muskrat fur
Hackle: Blue-dun hen

Little Olive Flymph
Hook: Standard dry fly, #14–#18
Thread: Olive 6/0
Tail: Blue-dun hen-hackle fibers
Rib: Narrow gold tinsel
Body: Olive fur
Hackle: Blue-dun hen

Brown Hackle
Hook: Standard dry fly, #10–#16
Thread: Red 6/0
Rib: Narrow gold tinsel
Body: Peacock herl
Hackle: Furnace

SOFT-HACKLE WETS

March Brown Spider
Hook: Standard dry fly, #10–#16
Thread: Orange 6/0
Rib: Narrow gold tinsel
Body: Hare's mask fur
Hackle: Brown partridge

Partridge and Yellow
Hook: Standard dry fly, #10–#16
Thread: Yellow 6/0
Body: Yellow floss
Thorax: Hare's mask fur
Hackle: Gray partridge

Partridge and Green
Hook: Standard dry fly, #10–#16
Thread: Green 6/0
Body: Green floss
Thorax: Hare's mask fur
Hackle: Gray partridge

Appendix D:
Streamers and Bucktails

Black-Nose Dace
Hook: 6XL, #4–#12
Thread: Black 6/0
Tail: Red wool yarn
Body: Embossed silver tinsel
Underwing: White bucktail
Midwing: Black bear hair
Overwing: Brown bucktail

Mickey Finn
Hook: 6XL, #4–#12
Thread: Black 6/0
Body: Embossed silver tinsel
Underwing: Yellow bucktail
Midwing: Red bucktail
Overwing: Yellow bucktail

Streamers. Row 1 (left to right): Black-Nose Dace, Mickey Finn, Royal Coachman Bucktail, Little Brown Trout. Row 2: Little Rainbow Trout, Little Brook Trout, Muddler Minnow. Row 3: Olive Woolly Bugger, Black Woolly Bugger, Black Marabou Muddler. *Andrew E. Cier*

Royal Coachman Bucktail
Hook: 6XL, #4–#12
Thread: Black 6/0
Tail: Golden pheasant tippets
Body: Peacock herl/red floss/peacock herl
Hackle: Coachman brown
Wing: White bucktail

Little Brown Trout
Hook: 6XL, #4–#12
Thread: Black 6/0
Tail: Bronze ringneck pheasant breast feather
Rib: Copper wire
Body: Cream fur
Underwing: Yellow bucktail
Midwing: Reddish orange bucktail
Overwing: Gray squirrel tail
Topping: Red squirrel tail
Cheek: Jungle cock or substitute

Little Rainbow Trout
Hook: 6XL, #4–#12
Thread: Black 6/0
Tail: Bright green bucktail
Rib: Flat silver tinsel
Body: Pale pink fur
Throat: Pink bucktail
Underwing: White bucktail
Midwing: Pink bucktail
Overwing: Bright green bucktail
Topping: Gray squirrel tail
Cheek: Jungle cock or substitute

Little Brook Trout
Hook: 6XL, #4–#12
Thread: Black 6/0
Tail: Red floss and bright green bucktail
Rib: Flat silver tinsel
Body: Cream fur
Throat: Orange bucktail
Underwing: White bucktail
Midwing: Orange bucktail
Overwing: Bright green bucktail
Topping: Gray squirrel tail
Cheek: Jungle cock or substitute

Muddler Minnow
Hook: 3XL, #2/0–#10
Thread: Brown
Weight: 10–15 turns lead wire, optional
Tail: Mottled turkey quill
Body: Flat gold tinsel
Underwing: Gray squirrel tail
Overwing: Mottled turkey quill
Hackle: Deer-hair collar
Head: Deer hair, spun and clipped

Olive Woolly Bugger
Hook: 3XL, #2/0–#10
Thread: Olive
Weight: 12–20 turns lead wire
Tail: Olive marabou
Hackle: Brown, palmered
Body: Olive chenille

Black Woolly Bugger
Hook: 3XL, #2/0–#10
Thread: Black
Weight: 12–20 turns lead wire
Tail: Black marabou
Hackle: Black, palmered
Body: Black chenille

Black Marabou Muddler
Hook: 3XL, #2/0–#10
Thread: Black
Weight: 12–20 turns lead wire
Tail: Black marabou
Body: Black fur
Wing: Black marabou
Hackle: Black deer-hair collar
Head: Black deer hair, spun and clipped

Bibliography

Bates, Joseph D., Jr. *Streamer Fly Tying and Fishing*. Harrisburg: Stackpole Books, 1966.

Bergman, Ray. *Trout*. New York: Alfred A. Knopf, 1938.

Borger, Gary A. *Nymphing*. Harrisburg: Stackpole Books, 1979.

Brooks, Charles. *The Trout and the Stream*. New York: Crown Publishers, 1974.

———. *Nymph Fishing For Larger Trout*. New York: Crown Publishers, 1976.

Brooks, Joe. *Trout Fishing*. New York: Outdoor Life Books, 1972.

Caucci, Al, and Bob Nastasi. *Hatches*. New York: Comparahatch Press, 1975.

Curtis, Brian. *The Life Story of the Fish*. New York: Dover, 1949.

Cutcliffe, H. C. *The Art of Trout Fishing on Rapid Streams*. South Molton, 1863.

Goddard, John, and Brian Clarke. *The Trout and the Fly*. New York: Nick Lyons Books, 1980.

Hafele, Rick, and Dave Hughes. *The Complete Book of Western Hatches*. Portland: Frank Amato Publications, 1981.

Heacox, Cecil E. *The Complete Brown Trout.* New York: Winchester Press, 1974.

Hidy, Vernon S. *Wet-Fly Fishing.* Philadelphia and New York: J. B. Lippincott, 1961.

Hughes, Dave. *American Fly Tying Manual.* Portland: Frank Amato Publications, 1986.

———. *Western Streamside Guide.* Portland: Frank Amato Publications, 1987.

———. *Handbook of Hatches.* Harrisburg: Stackpole Books, 1987.

———. *Reading the Water.* Harrisburg: Stackpole Books, 1988.

———. *Tackle and Technique For Taking Trout.* Harrisburg: Stackpole Books, 1990.

Humphreys, Joseph B. *Joe Humphrey's Trout Tactics.* Harrisburg: Stackpole Books, 1981.

LaFontaine, Gary. *Caddisflies.* New York: Winchester Press/Nick Lyons Books, 1981.

Lee, Art. *Fishing Dry Flies for Trout on Rivers and Streams.* New York: Atheneum, 1983.

Leisenring, James E., and Vernon S. Hidy. *The Art of Tying the Wet Fly and Fishing the Flymph.* New York: Crown Publishers, 1971.

Lusch, Ed. *Comprehensive Guide to Western Gamefish.* Portland: Frank Amato Publications, 1985.

McClane, A. J. *McClane's Standard Fishing Encyclopedia.* New York: Holt, Rinehart, and Winston, 1965.

Marinaro, Vince. *A Modern Dry Fly Code.* New York: Crown Publishers, 1950.

———. *In the Ring of the Rise.* New York: Nick Lyons Books, 1976.

Migel, J. Michael, Editor. *The Masters on the Dry Fly.* New York: Nick Lyons Books, 1989.

———, and Leonard M. Wright, Jr., Editors. *The Masters on the Nymph.* New York: Nick Lyons Books, 1979.

Nemes, Sylvester. *The Soft-Hackled Fly.* Old Greenwich: Chatham Press, 1975.

Ovington, Ray. *Tactics on Trout.* New York: Alfred A. Knopf, 1969.

———. *How to Take Trout on Wet Flies and Nymphs.* Rockville Center: Freshet Press, 1974.

———. *Commonsense Fly Fishing.* Harrisburg: Stackpole Books, 1983.

Proper, Datus. *What the Trout Said.* New York: Nick Lyons Books, 1989.

Ronalds, Alfred. *The Fly-Fisher's Entomology.* London: 1836.

Rosborough, E. H. *Tying and Fishing the Fuzzy Nymphs.* Harrisburg: Stackpole Books, 1988.

Schwiebert, Ernest. *Trout.* New York: E. P. Dutton, 1978.

———. *Nymphs.* New York: Winchester Press, 1973.

Skues, G. E. M. *The Way of a Trout with a Fly.* London: A. & C. Black, 1921.

Smith, Robert H. *Native Trout of North America.* Portland: Frank Amato Publications, 1984.

Stewart, W. C. *The Practical Angler.* London: A. & C. Black, 1857.

Swisher, Doug, and Carl Richards. *Selective Trout.* New York: Crown, 1971.

———. *Fly Fishing Strategy.* New York: Crown, 1975.

Tod, E. M. *Wet-Fly Fishing.* London: Sampson Low, Marston & Co., 1914.

Trotter, Patrick C. *Cutthroat.* Boulder: Colorado Associated University Press, 1987.

Wright, Leonard M., Jr. *Fishing the Dry Fly as a Living Insect.* New York: E. P. Dutton, 1972.

Index